COUNTY DURHAM
Strange but True

ROBERT WOODHOUSE

The History Press

First published in 2004 by Sutton Publishing

Reprinted in 2009 by
The History Press
The Mill, Brimscombe Port,
Stroud, Gloucestershire, GL5 2QG
www.thehistorypress.co.uk

Reprinted 2014

**British Library Cataloguing in
Publication Data**
A catalogue record for this book is available
from the British Library.

ISBN 978-0-7509-3731-3

Typeset in 11/13 Photina.
Typesetting and origination by
Sutton Publishing Limited.
Printed and bound in Great Britain by
Marston Book Services Limited, Oxfordshire

Mr William Staley of Underhurth Farm, Forest in Teesdale, photographed at Middleton-in-
Teesdale after walking 7 miles with his shorthorn cow on the way to the railway station.

Contents

Castellated colliery buildings in the Washington area.

Introduction

Each area of Britain has a common set of historical threads that have determined the overall nature of both the rural and the urban landscapes. Significant national trends in terms of architectural styles, land use and industrial enterprises have all played a part in shaping the overall appearance of an area, but throughout each location it is the range of local influences, both natural and man-made, that provides a distinctive and often highly unusual flavour.

The north-east's importance as an early Christian centre is reflected in St Cuthbert's connections with Jarrow and the city of Durham as well as sites at Norton-on-Tees, while successive bishops of Durham have left their mark not only

The French-style town hall at Bishop Auckland.

The Bowes Museum at Barnard Castle.

in religious and military fields but also in architectural terms. Other prominent local landmarks were the work of landed families such as the Lambtons or Lumleys, and it was the Bowes family's connection with France that brought a splendid French-style chateau to the heart of Teesdale.

The area's geological formation, with rich mineral deposits, led to the late-nineteenth-century growth of spa resorts and the protracted scheme for a canal from coalfields to the coast, while the county's coastline not only harboured Peter Allen's family at Marsden but also prompted plans for town walls at Hartlepool and the curious tale of the ill-fated monkey.

With such a varied background, it is perhaps only to be expected that County Durham should provide such a fascinating and remarkable selection of extraordinary people, places and incidents.

All photographs in the book are from the Beamish Photographic Archive or the personal collection of the author, apart from those on pp. 104 and 105, which are from the collection of Mrs C. Hanley.

1 Extraordinary People

Every area has its own collection of extraordinary characters. Some personalities contribute to the local scene by adding colour, interest and endless talking points. Others add to nationally important fields of knowledge and a few make a memorable mark in foreign fields.

One of Sunderland's best-loved characters from earlier days must be Tommy Sanderson. Well known throughout the Wearside area, he led a colourful existence from an unusual base in an iron hut, which he named 'Metal Hall'. Numbered among his writings are a volume of verse called *Freaks of Fancy* and an autobiography *Chips and Shavings of an Old Shipwright* in which he described the town as he knew it during his childhood. Tommy Sanderson is probably best remembered as Sunderland's last town crier and his bell is lodged in the splendid museum building. He died in 1892.

Allensford Bridge over the River Derwent, close to the home of Thomas Thompson.

Other personalities preferred quieter rural parts and Thomas Thompson chose to follow a solitary lifestyle in the upper reaches of the Derwent Valley near Allensford. This 'Old Man of the Woods' lived out an existence in a ramshackle dwelling and is perhaps best remembered for his habit of reading a Bible while sitting in a coffin.

Thomas Thompson, hermit in the Derwent Valley,
reading a Bible while sitting in his coffin.

The village of Hurworth, near Darlington, was the birthplace of William Emerson, in 1701. His father was a schoolmaster but it seems that young Emerson had little interest in academic matters until his later teenage years. After completing his studies in Newcastle and York, he returned to Hurworth to set up a school of his own, but William Emerson's fiery temperament was unsuited to teaching and the school soon closed. He then travelled to London, where he found work writing a series of manuals for mathematics students and producing articles under the pen-name of 'Merones' (a rearrangement of his own surname) and a pseudonym to end all pseudonyms – Philofluentmechanalgegeomast!

Returning to his home village of Hurworth, Emerson married the niece of Dr Johnson, the local rector. Part of the wedding arrangements was payment of a dowry of £500, but when this sum was not handed over an unhappy William

Emerson Arms, Hurworth, celebrating the life and achievements
of the local mathematician and magician, William Emerson.

A window of the Emerson Arms, showing William Emerson's date of birth (1701),
one of his pseudonyms, 'Merones', and the date of alterations to the building (1909).

Washington Hall, early home of Gertrude Bell,
an extraordinary diplomatist and explorer.

Emerson approached the rector about the matter. He was met with a blunt refusal and responded by bundling all his wife's clothing and personal belongings into a wheelbarrow and then dumping them on the vicarage doorstep.

During 1743 Emerson's first successful work, *Doctrine of Fluxions*, was published and this was followed by *Mechanics and Methods of Increments*. These books increased both his income and his reputation as a mathematician, and in the local neighbourhood William Emerson was gaining increasing credit as a magician. He certainly had the look of a man of wizardry with coarse shirts worn back to front and underneath old sleeveless waistcoats. His wigs were unkempt and topped by battered, trimmed-down hats.

Regular Monday visits to Darlington market extended into 48-hour absences from home as Emerson indulged in rounds of conversation and drinking with his cronies. His manner and vocabulary were abrupt and forthright and an offer of membership of the Royal Society was met by a disdainful dismissal.

During his later life William Emerson took up angling and spent long periods standing waist deep in the waters of the Tees. He made a surprising claim that this routine was very beneficial to his gout. After spending time helping some of his students construct a boat, he is said to have found it highly amusing when the vessel and its young crew sank to the riverbed shortly after being launched.

William Emerson, mathematician, magician and eccentric angler, died on 21 May 1782 at the age of 81 and is buried along with his long-suffering wife close to the west door of the parish church.

Until recent years it was difficult for women to make their mark in most walks of life, but during the late nineteenth and early twentieth centuries a remarkable woman from County Durham distinguished herself not only as an academic but also as an adventurer and international representative. Born in 1868 at Washington Hall, Gertrude Bell was daughter of Sir Thomas Bell, the well-known north-east ironmaster, and granddaughter of Sir Lowthian Bell. Before the age of 20, during 1887, she gained a first-class honours degree in modern history from Oxford University and soon displayed outstanding bravery and skill during mountaineering expeditions to the Alps. These talents were utilised in full when she turned her attention to the Middle East, where journeys into Syria and Palestine were followed, during 1913, by an expedition into the depths of Arabia. She travelled some 550 miles across Arabian deserts as far as Hail, in the centre of Arabia, before local tribesmen stopped her from going further south because of their civil war with neighbouring groups. Turning northwards, Gertrude Bell journeyed for more than 450 miles to reach Baghdad, befriending nomadic Arabs on the way to completing one of the greatest overland journeys by a lone woman explorer.

During the First World War Gertrude Bell's knowledge of the tribesmen of northern Arabia proved invaluable to British intelligence officers and after the war her knowledge of the area and intellectual ability ensured that she played a major role in shaping the future of Middle Eastern states. She went to Mesopotamia as Secretary to the British Commissioner and played a leading role in delicate and complicated negotiations with local Arabs. Geographical boundaries were being drawn up and it was because of Gertrude Bell's advice and influence that the Emir Feisal became King of Iraq.

Once diplomatic work was completed she decided to make a permanent home in Iraq, where she played a major role in establishing a national museum in the capital, Baghdad. This remarkable woman from Washington, County Durham, died in 1926 and is buried in the English cemetery at Baghdad.

Another local woman has found a place in history books for rather different reasons. Margaret Nicholson was born at Stockton-on-Tees in 1750 and spent much of her early life as a housemaid before moving to London, where she spent some three years in lodgings on the corner of Wigmore Street, Marylebone. She is said to have made a living by taking in needlework, but her attention was firmly focused on a claim to the throne of England. During July 1786 she sent a petition to the Privy Council on the subject of pretenders and usurpers to the throne, but it received no attention.

Soon afterwards, on 2 August, Margaret Nicholson was among a crowd of people at the garden entrance to St James's Palace as the king, George III, arrived back from Windsor. She presented a paper to him and then attempted to stab him with an old ivory-handled dessert knife. The knife passed through his waistcoat and bent against the skin. She was soon disarmed by an attendant and, but for the intervention of the King himself, she would have been attacked by the angry crowd. A messenger led her away into detention.

When her lodgings in Marylebone were searched, several letters to a number of prominent people were found and in these letters she claimed to have a right to the throne. On 8 August she appeared before the Privy Council and two doctors certified her as insane. She was committed to Bethlehem (or Bedlam) Hospital with the recommendation that she should work if she was in a fit state. Margaret Nicholson died in the hospital on 14 May 1828.

Down the years numerous tales have sprung up about Marsden Bay and adjacent cliff tops and figuring prominently among these are Peter Allen and his family. He was born at Tranent, East Lothian, and at an early age moved with his parents to the Whitburn area. After working for the Williamson family at Whitburn Hall, Peter Allen later became a publican in the area and also worked on local building projects. With an eye to business, he noted the number of visitors to the Marsden area and used his winnings from Shields races to sell refreshments to day trippers. He also spent time enlarging and excavating the caves to make a house in the cliff face, but then ran into problems for selling alcohol without a licence. Local magistrates eventually granted him a licence and the suspicions of Excise men about smuggling activities were laid to rest.

Marsden Rock and Grotto in 1955 with distant views of Whitburn village.

A view of Marsden Grotto in 1930. During the mid-nineteenth century
it was the home of Peter Allen and his family.

Peter Allen and his wife raised eight children at their home in the grotto,
where they survived hair-raising moments when gale force winds hurled North
Sea breakers through the door of the cave. During the winter of 1846 the
Allen family was isolated for six weeks in their shore-line dwelling among an
assortment of animals, birds and even bees.

During successive summer seasons visitors arrived at Marsden by road,
steamship and on foot and inevitably there were dramatic incidents of rescue
when young and old were trapped by incoming tides. Peter Allen and his family
spent some twenty-two years at the grotto before their claim to occupy the
caves was challenged by John Clay, owner of the nearby Marsden Rock Farm.
The resulting court case and settlement at Durham Assizes in 1850 took a
toll on Peter Allen's health and he died on 31 August 1849 aged 51 years. He
was buried in Whitburn churchyard and it was left to other family members to
develop their home in the cave until 1974, when the tenancy expired.

2 Ecclesiastical Curiosities

Church buildings are fascinating from several points of view. They are essentially places of worship, but each one contains distinctive architectural features, monuments celebrating the lives of local worthies or church officials as well as a range of items relating to previous parish events. An adjacent churchyard often adds further interest with curious gravestones or unusual ancillary buildings.

The village of High Coniscliffe has mainly Georgian properties spreading along high ground overlooking the River Tees some 4 miles west of Darlington, and these give little indication of its early history. Reference is made in the Anglo-Saxon Chronicle to the death during 778 of a high sheriff named Eldulf at Ciningesclif, 'the King's Cliff'. The monarch in question was Edwin of Northumbria, to whom the church is dedicated, and it is the only one in England with this dedication. The present building has items of Saxon stonework in its walls and a Norman north doorway, but it was extensively restored and reroofed in 1846.

St Edwin's Church, High Coniscliffe.

11

St Mary's Church, Norton-on-Tees.

Central crossing tower, St Mary's Church, Norton-on-Tees.

St Mary's Church at Norton-on-Tees is the only cruciform Saxon church in the north of England and the central tower and transepts remain largely unaltered. Outstanding features of the Saxon tower are the eight triangular-headed little windows, several of which are formed of single stones, and the four round-headed arches, 7ft high and 2ft wide. Arches on the north and south sides still display their original rugged simplicity. The others have fine mouldings dating from the late twelfth century. The clerestory and nave arcades also date from the late twelfth century. Built into the wall on the south side of the chancel arch is a fragment of a Saxon cross with an interlacing pattern, but the most impressive carving is an early fourteenth-century effigy under the tower. It shows an unknown knight sitting cross legged in chain armour with a sword fastened to his belt. Above his cushioned hand is a crocketed canopy, while at his feet a lion and dog fight furiously and on his right side sits a small female figure with an open book.

In the north transept is a marble monument to the Hogg family of Norton House (now demolished). The most prominent member of the family was Thomas Jefferson Hogg, friend and biographer of the poet Shelley. Located in the south-east corner of the churchyard is a headstone that has the inscription 'Sacred to the memory of John Walker, chymist and druggist . . . The original inventor of matches (friction lights)'. (His discovery was made at his chemist's shop on Stockton High Street during the late months of 1826.)

Hartlepool has two churches of great interest. The ancient parish church of St Hilda dominates the headland area, while the centre of Church Square in the former township of West Hartlepool is occupied by the incredible outlines of Christ Church. Ralph Ward Jackson, promoter of West Hartlepool, employed the unconventional mid-Victorian architect E.B. Lamb to carry out work, and designs were completed during 1850. Completion of the building, in 1854, represented Lamb's first important urban project and cemented his reputation as a 'rogue' architect. A tall west tower has an extraordinary mixture of architectural styles and completely dwarfs the low body of the church, which also displays an outlandish assortment of design work among internal roof timbers. It all adds up to an incredible example of church architecture, though in recent years it has taken on a different role as an information centre and art gallery.

The former mining village of Bowburn is located beside the A177 road to the south of Durham City and peeping over roof tops are the strange outlines of the Church of Christ the King. Constructed during the late 1960s to designs by Harold Wharfe of Newcastle University, it has been described as looking 'like a spaceship'. In terms of materials and architecture it is certainly out of the ordinary, with a composition that includes concrete panels, glass-fibre dome and a curious amalgam of cross with spire.

All Saints' Church at Penshaw was built in 1745 and altered in 1876–7 to designs by C.H. Fowler. During the Victorian renovations a monument was inserted into the fabric of the building in memory of the Elliot family and it is set apart from other memorials by the fact that it originally formed part of the Great

Christ Church, Church Square, Hartlepool.

Christ the King, Bowburn.

Pyramid of Gizeh, near Cairo. The pyramid incorporated the tomb of Cheops, who died some 6,500 years ago, and the block of stone was brought home by Sir George Elliot, MP, with permission from Ismail Pasha, Khedive of Egypt.

St Mary's Church at West Rainton, between Durham and Sunderland, was erected in 1864, but the prominent 130ft spire was added a few years later in 1877. A tablet in the church has an inscription stating that the tower and spire were the gift of Sir George Elliot in thanksgiving for his safe return from Egypt. (As at Penshaw, the tablet was part of a block from the Great Pyramid of Gizeh.)

Many churches have monuments celebrating the lives and achievements of local noble families and often they are on a grand scale, but one of the Lambton memorials at Burnmoor Church deserves special mention. The church itself was built by the Second Earl of Durham and dedicated in 1868. Internal decoration was added in 1881 by Johnson and Hicks, but it is the huge marble figure of Nike – a winged Angel of Victory – that catches the attention. Located in the north aisle, it was carved at Rome in 1894 by Waldo Storey and celebrates the lives of the Third Earl of Durham and his twin brother, who was briefly Fourth Earl. This amazing sculpture was installed in the church by the Fifth Earl during 1929.

A very different item is to be found against the south wall of the sanctuary at St Paul's Church, Jarrow. Traditionally known as 'Bede's Chair', but probably dating from the fourteenth century, it has been heavily mutilated down the years as expectant and superstitious mothers have chipped away good-luck charms. (The venerable Bede spent much of his life in the monastery on this site that was founded by his tutor Benedict Biscop.)

The first buildings at Finchale Priory were completed by a hermit, St Godric, in about 1110. He died in 1170 and some ten years later it became a rest house for monks from nearby Durham. Down the years stories have been told about the value to barren women of praying at the shrine of St Godric. The tales suggested that, after praying for children at the shrine, women pilgrims were invited to visit the Prior's Parlour, where there was a large oriel window in the north wall. At this location they were directed to kneel facing the window and to pray resolutely for a child, while ignoring any external sounds, movements or touches. In fact these contacts were to be welcomed as proof that St Godric was purging their bodies of the devils who had rendered them infertile. When the bell for Prime sounded, female pilgrims were directed from the Prior's Parlour into the church, where they gave thanks to St Godric for his intervention.

The Church of St Mary and St Cuthbert at Chester-le-Street has several unusual features, including one of the best-preserved anchorages (or anker houses) in the country, the finest church spire within the county and an amazing array of effigies along the wall of the north aisle.

An anchorite (recluse) lived in this curious little stone building from 1383 until the Dissolution, when it was occupied by four poor widows. In 1626 a

Left:
St Paul's
Church,
Jarrow.

Right:
Altar and
choir stalls
of St Paul's
Church,
Jarrow.

Finchale Priory near Durham City.

Engraving of the Prior's Lodging at Finchale Priory.

curate attempted to evict them and went as far as obtaining a warrant from Durham to give them a ducking. According to reports, the women enlisted the help of three strong men and added 'a barr to the inner door' in order to ensure their continued residence. The anchorage itself consists of two rooms on the ground floor and two more above. A narrow slit in the wall of the upper floor allowed the anchorite to see the altar in the south aisle of the main church and another opening allowed food to be passed to him from the tower.

The spire dates from about 1400 and rises 189ft from an octagonal base on top of an early English tower. Beneath the tower is an array of effigies known locally as 'Lumley's Warriors' because they were installed in 1594 by John, Seventh Lord Lumley. Fourteen figures make up this aisle of tombs and at the west end the walls display details of this proud family's history. Only five are genuine Lumley effigies; others were imported from dissolved monasteries and several were specially carved for the display. (Two genuine family effigies were removed under licence from the graveyard of Durham Cathedral.) In order to accommodate all the figures, Lord Lumley had to cut the feet off some effigies.

The Church of St Mary and St Cuthbert, Chester-le-Street.

19

As well as adding solemnity and dignity to main church buildings, churchyards often have their own features of interest. St Mary's Church at Middleton-in-Teesdale was completed in 1878 to designs by C. Hodgson Fowler, but across the churchyard on the northern side is an unusual detached bell house (or belfry). Constructed in 1567, it represents the only detached belfry within the old boundaries of County Durham and was built to house three bells. Funding for this intriguing little building was provided by a parson named William Bele. The three bells could be rung by one man using two hands and a foot.

Right: The detached bell house in the churchyard at Middleton-in-Teesdale.

Below: The old church at Middleton-in-Teesdale. The detached bell house is in the distance on the left of the photograph. This church was demolished and replaced by the present St Mary's Church.

The grave of Mark Harold Casper in Hartlepool cemetery,
showing the carved stone violin on the gravestone.

Gravestones provide valuable information for social historians and genealogists and some include unusual, but wholly appropriate, symbols or decorations. The grave of Mark Harold Casper (born 18 October 1889, buried 11 July 1908) in Hartlepool cemetery is decorated with a carved stone violin. A group of yew trees in Lamesley churchyard surround the headstone of John Turner, a shipwright from South Shields, who died in 1811. At the top of the stone is a striking carving of a ship ready for launching with a flag flying from its stern. In the same churchyard is the grave of John Croft, vicar of Lamesley from 1898 until his death in 1951. Some two years earlier, at the age of 98, he had fallen from a ladder while pruning fruit trees; as he recovered Revd Croft is said to have reread the New Testament in Greek. During 1950 he and his wife celebrated their seventy-fifth wedding anniversary.

Haughton-le-Skerne churchyard holds reminders of an episode that became known as the Great Burdon Poisoning Mystery. Just a few feet from the church tower lies the grave of Joseph Snaith Wooler, who died on 25 September 1871 at the age of 61. It also marks the final resting place of his wife, Jane, who died some years earlier on 27 June 1855 aged 46 years. These two people became the central characters in the sequence of events that followed. Contemporary reports state that Mr and Mrs Wooler had spent many years in India before returning to the Darlington area, and soon after her burial there were rumours that she had been poisoned. A subsequent examination of her remains established the presence of arsenic and, as suspicion pointed towards a case of systematic, slow poisoning, her husband, Joseph Wooler, was arrested and charged with murder. Mr Wooler's innocence was established with evidence from Sergeant Wilkins, who pointed out that it was the custom for ladies in India to take small doses of arsenic in order to improve their complexions. Following his acquittal, Joseph Wooler spent the last sixteen years of his life at Haughton and was buried in the same grave as his late wife.

Local records point to a clandestine marriage at Haughton when William Emmerson was charged at Durham Court on 11 July 1633. He admitted that he had been married by an unknown stranger in one of his barns. His punishment was to acknowledge his wrongdoing while wearing a penitential habit, either in the parish church at Haughton or at the market cross in Durham City. A fine totalling £100 was also imposed, but in the event he was released after paying costs of just £9.

An unusual building is located to the rear of Stanhope Church, where a hearse house is incorporated into the wall of the churchyard.

The graveyard at Muggleswick marks the final resting place of a giant hunter, Edward Ward. His favourite hound is said to have had a litter of puppies in one of his outsize wooden shoes.

A hearse house at the rear of Stanhope churchyard.

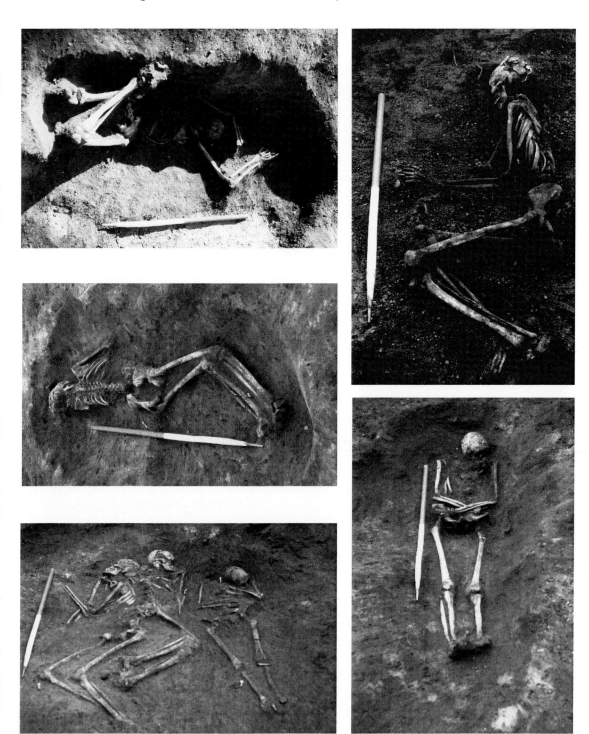

Examples of Anglo-Saxon burials, dating from the seventh century AD
and found at sites in the Norton area.

On the subject of graveyards and burials, discoveries at Norton, north of Stockton-on-Tees, have unearthed a fascinating sequence of cemeteries. During the early 1980s a pagan cemetery was excavated close to the site of the former Norton Mill and investigations revealed about 125 burials dating from the period AD 550–610. Four main types of burial were uncovered: extended burials, the most common, with bodies stretched out in the grave and lying on their backs; crouched burials, much less common, with people placed on this sides as if asleep; prone burials, where bodies appear face down after being thrown headfirst into the grave with their hands and feet tied together (making it likely that these people may have been buried alive as a punishment for cowardice or witchcraft); and cremation burials, where cremated remains had been placed in small urns. One of the urns had been placed in a pit on top of some animal bones. It contained the remains of two people, an adult and a teenager. A rare discovery was a male burial with a spear and wooden bucket (fashioned from a yew tree and decorated with bronze bands), indicating the high status of the male.

During the mid-1990s further human remains were discovered at Bishopsmill School, some 200 yards from the pagan cemetery. Extensive investigation of this site in 2003 exposed a total of 83 graves and 107 individuals, with most lying east–west. Several of the graves contained iron artefacts in the shape of small hinge straps and corner brackets from wooden chests. Some of these had iron locks, and an iron key was found at the foot of one of the bodies. During his or her lifetime each person would have owned a wooden chest to store personal possessions; after death, belongings would be divided up and the chest used as a coffin. Chest fittings of this type are comparatively rare and the nearest examples previously discovered were at Ripon and York.

The cemetery at Bishopsmill School dates from the arrival of Christianity in the Teesside area during the early 600s and probably started at the time when the nearby pagan cemetery went out of use. It is believed to contain at least 600 individuals and probably continued in use until the present church building was brought into use during the 1080s. The size of the cemetery may indicate that it served the whole parish of Norton, which included Stockton, Hartburn and Preston, and it is highly likely that there was a church in the immediate locality.

Recent investigations of the two Anglo-Saxon burial sites, along with consideration of the current churchyard (around St Mary's Church), show a fascinating progression of cemeteries dating from about 600 to the present day and moving in an east–west direction.

After the death of St Cuthbert of Lindisfarne, his body was brought to Durham and a magnificent cathedral took shape over his shrine. It was planned to include a Lady Chapel in the usual position at the east end of the cathedral, but builders encountered so many structural problems that the project was abandoned. The feeling at the time was that St Cuthbert was expressing his disapproval and consequently Durham is the only cathedral in England with a Lady Chapel at the wrong end, by the west door.

3 Follies

Definitions of these curious buildings range from 'a great useless structure' to 'an architectural joke'. Such flights of architectural fancy were sometimes inspired by the fantasies of rich and powerful men, while other mystical monuments served a practical use or celebrated noteworthy events and achievements.

Successive bishops of Durham since the twelfth century have been based at Bishop Auckland, where buildings spread along a natural ridge between the rivers Wear and Gaunless with adjacent parkland running eastwards away from the township. Considerable damage was caused to the bishop's residence, Auckland Castle, during the dramatic events of the English Civil War and subsequent occupation from 1647 to 1657 by Sir Arthur Hazelrigg, Governor of the North, so that the existing buildings show design work carried out by later bishops. Bishop Cosin began the process of renovation with a mixture of Gothic and Restoration styles, and during the 1750s Bishop Trevor added contemporary Gothic features (both here at Bishop Auckland and at his other main residence, Durham Castle). Further decorative touches were added by Bishop Egerton, and during Bishop Barrington's period of office (1749–56) the design skills of James Wyatt were employed to unify the overall scheme.

The deer house built by Bishop Richard Trevor in the deer park of Auckland Castle.

Bishop Richard Trevor's work included the addition of an elaborate gatehouse built in 1760, with design work by Sir Thomas Robinson of Rokeby near Barnard Castle. His playful approach to architectural detail produced an assortment of battlements, decorative pinnacles and four-petalled flowers (quatrefoils) and this mood of Gothic-style gaiety continues in the screen wall and inner gateway of 1796.

Away from the main range of buildings, parkland was redesigned during the early 1750s. Its most striking feature, a deer house (built 1767), is located on a ridge above the River Gaunless and incorporates all the basic creature comforts along with fanciful architectural details featured in the gatehouse (which had been completed seven years earlier). Deer sheltered in the roofed passageway between walls that ran along each side of the square structure and a tall tower on the west side allowed viewing of the animals. Outer walls were arcaded; pinnacles, decorated corners and a central tower, with cross arrow slits and quatrefoils (four-petalled flowers), completed the fanciful architectural detail.

On a smaller scale, and with less ornamental detail, there is another Gothic-style deer house in the grounds of the Hall Garth Country House Hotel at Coatham Mundeville, on Darlington's northern outskirts. The corner turrets and stone-faced frontage feature cruciform arrow slits and above the double-arched Tudor entrance is a stepped gable. Ranking as one of the most attractive of all deer houses, it now makes an ideal backdrop for wedding groups from the nearby hotel. Hardwick Country Park at Sedgefield is the setting for County Durham's finest collection of eighteenth-century follies. The blend of natural and man-made features was created during the 1750s when the owner, John Burdon, called on the design

The central tower and a pinnacled corner of the deer house.

The summerhouse at Hardwick Hall, Sedgefield.

skills of James Paine and a local architect, John Bell, to transform his 150-acre estate into parkland that reflected contemporary landscape trends.

A lake covered the valley below Hardwick Hall, and located around the serpentine canal that fed into the lake were seven buildings among areas of woodland. Three of these splendid structures have disappeared completely: the Banqueting House, which was the showpiece, with busts of Vitruvius, Inigo Jones and Palladio (originator of the Palladian style of architecture; the Doric Bath House, with its façade to rival the exterior of Gibside Chapel; and the Gothic Seat, with its ogee (S-shaped) windows. Of the four remaining buildings, only one classical one, the superb Temple of Minerva, survives, even though much of it has been dismantled and bricked up. Until recent years remaining features around the estate have seemed to be facing demolition.

Durham County Council purchased the site (excluding the hall) in 1972 and early phases of improvement focused on the parkland, but during the early 1990s the Gothic-style gateway was repaired and the serpentine bridge was fully restored. Further restoration work highlighted the gateway arch, partly made up with fragments of stone from Guisborough Priory, and rebuilt the round tower to about half its original height (of 50ft).

During 2003 the award of a £4 million National Lottery grant facilitated the start of work (in September 2003) on a ten-year restoration scheme. Other aspects of the first phase of the scheme include excavation and restoration of the ornamental lake, renovation of the Temple of Minerva, the Gothic Seat, the grand terrace and the circuit walk. A heritage resource centre, car park and

- PENSHAW Mo
ERECTED TO THE MEMORY OF JO
WHO DIED IN 1840, FOR DISTINGUIS
FOUNDATION STONE LAID AUG. 28th 1:
THE DESIGN IS COPIED FROM THE T
DIMENSIONS - LENGTH 100 FT - WI
DIAMETER - HEIGHT 70 FT AT ONE E

Penshaw Monument at Penshaw Hill, celebrating the life of the First Earl of Durham.

MENT ~

GEORGE LAMBTON, EARL OF DURHAM.

SERVICE RENDERED TO HIS COUNTY.

BY THOMAS, EARL OF ZETLAND

OF THESIUS BUT DOUBLE THE

53FT - 18 COLUMNS EACH 6FT 6INS

AND 62FT AT THE OTHER END

new entrance will cater for the anticipated increase in visitors to this amazing collection of ornamental structures.

From a group of classical buildings to a single imposing feature: Penshaw Monument crowns the summit of a hill at the heart of former coalmining country and celebrates the life and achievement of John George Lambton, First Earl of Durham, and first Governor of Canada. Designed by local architects, John and Benjamin Green, this half-sized version of the Theseum in Athens was paid for with subscriptions from local people following the earl's death in 1840. Building work was completed in 1844 and comprises seven columns along the length, with four across either end. This incredible structure never had a roof, but a staircase in one of the huge columns (now closed) gave access to a parapet walkway. Industrial activity in the area not only blackened the stonework but also weakened the basic structure (through mine workings), and during 1996 the National Trust spent in excess of £100,000 on restoration work.

While the dramatic outlines of the Penshaw Monument celebrate the achievements of a nationally renowned radical politician, a much smaller Doric-style temple in Durham City provides a link with a much humbler but no less interesting personality. During the late nineteenth century a Polish dwarf, 'Count' Joseph Boruwlaski, visited Durham and decided to make his permanent home in the city. Measuring just 39in (99cm) in height, this amazing character, who was of noble birth but without an official title, spent much of his early life in the company of some of Europe's leading personalities. Voltaire, Maria Theresa of Austria and King George III took a close interest in this curious little man, but eventually he had to resort to giving musical concerts. During 1788 his memoirs were published in French – with English and German translations bringing further attention. Durham Cathedral authorities gave him a home, Bank's Cottage, close to the River Wear, and, although this building has been demolished, a small temple with Doric columns and a single room survives intact. Known as the Count's House, it has been used in recent years as a setting for open-air productions of ancient Greek plays.

Count Boruwlaski died in 1837 aged 97 and was buried in a simple grave at the west end of Durham Cathedral's north aisle. Carved into a little square are the initials 'J.B.' and a tiny cross. He had already written an appropriate epitaph:

> Poland was my cradle
> England is my nest
> Durham is my quiet place
> Where my bones shall rest

Other reminders of this curious little man were put on display in the lobby of the magistrates' court, where a statue and painting of Count Boruwlaski could be seen alongside his black suit, white stockings, shoes, embroidered hat box, cane and violin.

The Count's House, residence of Count Boruwlaski,
on the bank of the River Wear at Durham.

The Count's House was attached to Bank's Cottage,
which has since been demolished.

Some monuments can be said to achieve the status of follies when they are relocated in wholly inappropriate settings. The tall Doric column in the gardens of Edleston House at Gainford was originally erected at Stanwick Park near Richmond in celebration of the Peace of Aachen in 1748. It had been commissioned by Hugh Smithson Percy, First Earl of Northumberland, and was moved to its present site (along with a summerhouse) when Stanwick was demolished in 1923.

The imposing obelisk in the grounds of Wynyard Park (near Stockton-on-Tees) is linked with an intriguing tale of personality clashes between leading political figures. Standing to a height of 127ft the monument was erected in 1827 to mark the Duke of Wellington's visit to Wynyard. After his successes on the battlefield, the 'Iron Duke' became a major parliamentary personality, and the Marquis of Londonderry was proud to count himself among Wellington's close associates. Accordingly, the obelisk was inscribed with the words 'Wellington, Friend of Londonderry', but Londonderry's unstable temperament did not always find favour with the duke and the marquis was not given a seat in Wellington's cabinet of 1828. Londonderry's response was to shorten the inscription to a single-word statement – 'Wellington'. There was recompense for Londonderry in 1852, when the Order of the Garter, which had become vacant on Wellington's death, was conferred on him.

Two prominent landmarks on the South Durham landscape have had differing fortunes. Brusselton Folly, near Shildon, was demolished in the 1960s, but Westerton Folly has been restored by Durham University. The folly stands on a grassy ridge above the roadway through the village, which lies midway between Spennymoor and Bishop Auckland. This small, round stone tower with small buttresses, cross-shaped arrow slits and low doorway served a practical purpose, for it was built as an observatory by the eighteenth-century astronomer and mathematician Thomas Wright.

Born at Byers Green on 22 September 1711, Wright was educated in Bishop Auckland before taking up an apprenticeship with a watchmaker in the town. He left before his training was completed, spent a short time at sea and then worked as a teacher in Sunderland, before heading south to London. During the 1730s his skills as an astronomer led to the publication of an almanac for sailors and astronomers and the manufacture of scientific instruments for members of the nobility. In 1750 he turned down an invitation from the Russian court to take up the post of chief Professor of Navigation at St Petersburg University and produced his *Hypothesis of the Universe*, which included his theory on the nature of Saturn's rings and his thoughts about the paths of comets.

In 1756 Wright built a house at the end of Ghent Street, and, although the property was demolished in 1967, a plaque in the front garden makes reference to the importance of the site. A memorial window in the nearby St Peter's parish church, which celebrates the achievements of Thomas Wright, was dedicated by

Above: Westerton Folly at Westerton village near Spennymoor, built by the astronomer Thomas Wright.
Right and below: Brusselton Folly near Bishop Auckland, demolished in the 1960s.

Michael Turnbull, Bishop of Durham, on 19 September 1999. A commemorative plaque was added to the observatory tower in 1950 by the University of Durham – 200 years after publication of Wright's treatise *Hypothesis of the Universe*.

Building work on the tower started in 1780, but Thomas Wright died before it was completed and this could account for use of the term 'folly'. (Following his death on 22 February 1786 he was buried in St Andrew's churchyard at Bishop Auckland.) Inevitably, perhaps, speculation has grown up around the 'Wizard's Tower', with claims that he chose this grassy ridge as the site for his observatory because it was 700ft above sea level and because it was also the birthplace of his grandmother. A rather more fanciful story claims that the tower is linked to Durham Cathedral by a secret underground passage.

Any consideration of buildings resulting from flights of architectural fancy must include two more splendidly incongruous structures. There is a distinctly French tone to Bishop Auckland's Victorian town hall, which was built between 1860 and 1862 and occupies a prominent position on the east side of the marketplace. It may not be the sort of building that might be expected at the heart of a northern town, but there can be no doubt that it enriches and enlivens the townscape.

Then what about the magnificent Bowes Museum at Barnard Castle? Architect Jules Pellechet's masterpiece was scheduled for construction near Paris, but it was current unrest and instability that caused John Bowes, son of the Tenth Earl of Strathmore, to move it to a site near the Strathmore family home at Streatlam. It was built to house the collections of works of art, furniture and ceramics that had been amassed by John Bowes and his wife, the actress Josephine Benoite. Construction work began in 1869, but it was not officially opened until 1892, by which time both John and Josephine Bowes had died. In terms of size, scale and style it is quite out of keeping with this rural sector of County Durham, but the overstatement and incongruity only serve to enhance and increase the appeal of this majestic structure.

4 Failed Schemes

Familiar townscapes are constantly subject to change as new road systems, housing developments and regeneration schemes transform well-known locations. Even more intriguing are some of the over-ambitious projects that featured on drawing board and planning meeting . . . only to be abandoned before they saw the light of day.

Events surrounding the planning, construction and operations of the Stockton and Darlington Railway are well documented, but less well known is the earlier ambitious plan for a canal linking the Durham coalfields with the River Tees at Stockton. While engineers such as Brindley, Rennie and Smeaton directed construction work on major projects during the late eighteenth century, it was a local man, George Dixon, who experimented with a stretch of canal at Cockfield Fell near Raby Castle. His initial plans were to continue the waterway through

Cockerton Bridge on Darlington's western outskirts carried the 'Coal Road' over the Cocker Beck and stood close to the location of the planned canal and dock facilities.

Cockerton village green, close to the proposed canal and docks.

to the Tees at Barnard Castle or, in the long term, construct a canal through to the north-east coast. Local landowner the Earl of Darlington put paid to Dixon's plans in the Cockfield area, but he found considerable support from Darlington businessmen during a meeting at the town's Post House.

As a result of this gathering, James Brindley was appointed to survey a route from the Durham coalfield to the Tees and his proposals comprised a 33-mile-long canal (including three branch canals from Walworth to Piercebridge, Darlington to Croft and Coatham Stob to Yarm).

Measuring 16ft in width and 5ft 4in in depth, the total cost was estimated at £63,722. Apart from the huge expense involved, the major problem facing promoters of the scheme was the state of the Tees, where numerous obstacles faced vessels navigating the tortuous stretch from the North Sea to Stockton. Ships could take as long as three weeks negotiating the severe bends, sandbanks and rocky outcrops along this section of the river.

This early plan was soon shelved, but completion of the Mandale Cut in 1810 brought improved prospects. The 220yd-long canal removed a 2¼-mile loop in the Tees between Stockton and the river mouth. Construction work had been carried out by the Tees Navigation Company, and at the banquet to celebrate the opening of the route the company's solicitor, Leonard Raisbeck, suggested another appraisal of the earlier proposals. John Rennie was brought in to assess possible schemes and in 1812 he concluded that the original plan of 1767 remained the best option (although overall costs had risen to £95,600).

The collapse of Messrs Mowbray Hollingsworth Co. Bank on Darlington's High Row halted hopes of financial backing for the proposed canal during 1815, but just three years later Stockton-based Christopher Tennant detailed George Leather to draw up another scheme. Interested parties met in Stockton town hall on 7 July 1818 to hear Leather's plans for an alternative canal route from Stockton through Bishopton, Bradbury and Rushyford to Evenwood. Covering some 29 miles, it would include fifty locks to negotiate a drop in altitude of 442ft, and a width of 24ft at the southern end would double in size at the northern limit. A depth of 6ft would allow seagoing vessels to operate along the full length, but the total cost amounted to £205,283 (with a recommendation from Mr Leather that another 10 per cent should be added for 'incidents'!).

A total of eight collieries in the Shildon and Ferryhill area would be linked by canal to Stockton-on-Tees, but the neighbouring towns of Yarm and Darlington were set to lose out. As legal and financial planning continued in Stockton, Leonard Raisbeck was the only advocate of a railway instead of a canal system, and during the late summer of 1818 he transferred his allegiance to Darlington-

Cockerton village modern shopping precinct.

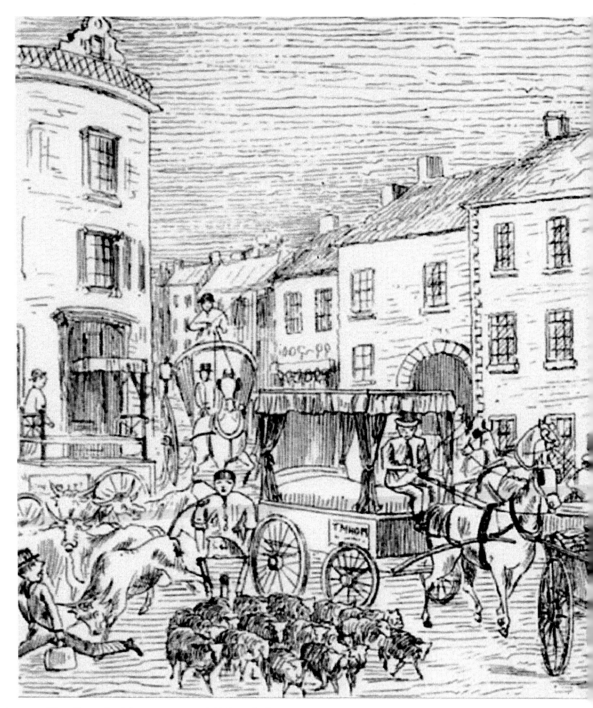

The Great Bed Movement in 1874 and the Banana Barge in 1953 prompted talk of shipments through the mythical Cockerton Docks.

based businessmen. The Darlington group commissioned John Rennie to review proposals and he suggested a rail link from collieries to Darlington with a canal from Darlington to Stockton. Another civil engineer, George Overton, then claimed that a railway was the best option and under Jonathan Backhouse's guidance Darlington's business fraternity threw their weight behind 'the Stockton and Darlington Railway'. A young Joseph Pease – aged 19 – drew up the prospectus for the new company and interested parties made financial contributions.

The Stockton group had gained support from the local landowner, Lord Stewart (later Lord Londonderry), but subscriptions of cash remained in short supply and on 24 December 1818 the committee announced an end to plans for a canal. The way was open for construction of the rail link.

A curious legacy of the canal scheme is the ongoing reference to Cockerton Docks on Darlington's western perimeter. There is no mention of the docks in an estimate of costs but they are shown on an engraved plan of the scheme. Wharves and warehouses would have been constructed beside the canal's route past Cockerton Bridge End.

A cottage on the south-east side of Elton village, close to the proposed new civil aerodrome for Stockton-on-Tees in the early 1930s.

In December 1953 the *Darlington and Stockton Times* carried a report of an incident with echoes of those mythical Cockerton Docks. A banana barge weighing 24 tonnes and measuring 70ft in length passed through Darlington's main streets on top of a pair of haulage tractors on the way to Africa. Guided through the town by a police escort, the slow-moving barge took just over half an hour to travel through Darlington before heading towards Catterick and eventually Liverpool.

Still on the subject of transport, and moving into the twentieth century, attention was firmly focused on flight by the 1930s. Much of the press coverage targeted development at Thornaby aerodrome, with particular attention paid to personnel, training and improved aircraft in 1935–6, but during 1930–1 there were dramatic moves in the field of civil aviation. On 8 January 1931 the *Middlesbrough Evening Gazette* reported on proposals for a municipal aerodrome at Stockton. Similar schemes were being put forward for other townships, including nearby Middlesbrough, and it seems that Stockton's Borough Engineer saw a 'great opportunity' for a civil airport on a site to the south of Darlington Road and bounded by Durham Lane, midway between the villages of Elton and Long Newton. The scheme failed to materialise and with the redevelopment of

An archway in the medieval town walls at Hartlepool, which were due to be replaced by a new set of town walls in the late sixteenth or early seventeenth centuries.

A length of medieval town wall around Hartlepool Headland,
where the proposed wall would extend.

Thornaby aerodrome site in the early 1960s it was the former wartime aerodrome of Goosepool at Middleton St George that was transformed into Teesside's civil airport.

During the late 1930s there was increasing talk of a threat from airborne forces, but some 300 years earlier local commanders' greatest fears were of invasion from the sea. Following the Rising of the North in 1569, when northern barons gave support to Mary Queen of Scots, and the subsequent siege of Barnard Castle, there was widespread alarm about the possible involvement of foreign troops. Rebel troops moved into Hartlepool during unrest surrounding the Rising of the North, but left before forces loyal to the Crown could organise a siege.

Reports of an Italian-looking stranger drawing plans of the townships and letters to Spain seeking armed assistance for local rebels served to increase fears of foreign invaders and strengthen calls for improved town walls at Hartlepool. Existing walls were constructed during the early fourteenth century during a period of Scottish raiding parties. Plans for replacement walls probably date from 1639, when Sir Thomas Morton viewed the state of defences and concluded that the medieval walls had fallen away in many places. Work on new defensive measures, he reported, would require charges and time to carry out repairs. The turbulent events of the English Civil War period and the expense involved probably account for the failure to make the planned changes and, ironically, Scottish forces occupied the township for three years from 1644.

5 All Things Great & Small

S ize may not really matter, but down the years attention has regularly focused on creatures or man-made features that fall into the categories of extremely large or surprisingly small.

Pride of place must go to the mighty Durham ox, which made headlines far and wide in the late eighteenth century. Robert Bakewell had attracted considerable attention to his farm at Dishley in Leicestershire, where he was employing methods of selective breeding to improve longhorn cattle. He died in 1795, but his methods were already being employed by farmers in County Durham. One of the early pioneers was Michael Dobinson of Sedgefield, who imported a bull from Holland in order to improve local shorthorn cattle, but other farmers were not as selective and early progress was brought to a standstill before a Mr Milbank of Barningham and a Mr Croft of Barford reared an animal that had great weight and also milked well.

The first documented example of the shorthorn or Tees Water Breed for size and weight was an ox owned by Mr Hill of Blackwell. It weighed 162 stones 10 pounds and was killed at Darlington on 17 December 1779 at the age of 7. These figures

The Blackwell ox, one of the famous breed of Durham shorthorn cattle.

Barmpton Hall, near Darlington, home of one of the Colling brothers,
who bred Durham shorthorn cattle.

Ketton Hall, home of Charles Colling, pioneering stockbreeder
in the late eighteenth and early nineteenth centuries.

44

The Colling Shorthorn Memorial Challenge Cup, presented by the Durham County Agricultural Committee to the Royal Agricultural Society of England in 1923.

The Comet public house at Hurworth Place, one of seventeen inns
named after a fine example of Durham shorthorn cattle.

were beaten almost ten years later when a 5-year-old ox owned by Mr Milbank
(of Barmingham) weighed in at 166 stone 4½ pounds when it was slaughtered at
Barnard Castle. Breeders were attempting to produce the greatest weight at the
earliest age and 5 years was considered to be the earliest age for slaughter.

The Colling brothers, Robert and Charles, who lived at Barmpton and Ketton
halls, farmed at the hamlet of Ketton on Darlington's north-eastern side and
became pioneering breeders of the Durham ox. Charles Colling is said to have
paid eight guineas for a bull from a neighbouring farmer. He named it 'Hubback'
and used it to breed Durham shorthorns. The Colling brothers hired out their
bulls for a year at a time in order to improve the quality of other herds at an
annual fee of between 50 and 100 guineas. One particularly fine specimen was
exhibited throughout England and Scotland between 1801 and 1807, drawing
appreciative crowds at each venue. A special carriage had been constructed to
transport the huge ox from place to place, but on 18 February 1807 disaster
struck during a visit to Oxford. The ox slipped and dislocated its hip bone and,
when there was no improvement in its condition, the beast had to be slaughtered
on 15 April. It was 11 years old and weighed an incredible 270 stones.

Throughout the area no fewer than seventeen public houses are still named
after this legendary beast. These include The Comet at Hurworth Place, close
to the northern end of Croft Bridge, where an appropriate signboard displays a
picture of the massive Durham ox.

The signboard of The Comet, Hurworth Place.

In human terms, John English was a true giant of a man. He arrived at Whickham, on the west side of Gateshead, during the 1830s, to work as a mason on the Scotswood suspension bridge and soon gained a reputation as a strong man. Standing around 6ft 5in tall, he soon earned the nickname 'Long Jack' and some of his alleged exploits only added to his legendary reputation. His party piece at Saturday night gatherings was to leap into the air and smash a hole in the ceiling with his head. On another occasion it is said that, when his pet dog was run over by a horse and wagon, he promptly picked up the wagon with its load of quarried stone and hurled it on its side along with the horse. A commemorative bust was sculpted in John English's lifetime by John Norvell.

We turn now from a giant to wee folk in the form of fairies at Bishopton near Stockton-on-Tees, where the local motte-and-bailey castle was known as 'Fairy Hill'. Set in low-lying marshy ground on the southern edge of the village, it was constructed in the twelfth century by the Conyers family, but village folk believed that it was home to fairies and their crock of gold.

The first phase of building work probably consisted of the mound and a defensive bank, which may have been completed by Roger de Conyers after he was given ownership of the Bishopton area in the early twelfth century. During 1141 the Bishopric of Durham was captured by William Cumin, with help from

Bishopton village.

Shafto family picnic at Bishopton Castle (known locally as Fairy Hill at one time) in 1915. The photograph shows the rear view of their Adler car.

Scottish forces, and Roger de Conyers led resistance to the occupation from his base at Bishopton. A second phase of building with defensive banks and ditches may date from this period and during 1143 his forces resisted an attack from rebel forces. The legitimate bishop, William de St Barbe, used Bishopton to launch his campaign to regain the bishopric and little is known about the site after the Conyers family moved to Sockburn, near Neasham.

As tales of the crock of gold persisted, local folk hatched a plan to excavate the site in search of the treasure. Digging deeper into the mound, so the tale continues, they eventually struck metal and in a frenzy of expectant excitement went on to uncover a metal box. Their attempts to force the lock were unsuccessful and the box was manhandled along to the local blacksmith, who was able to use the tools of his trade to prise open the heavy lid. Hopes of newly discovered treasure were soon dashed, as the 'treasure chest' proved to contain nothing more than a set of rusty old nails. If there is any element of truth in this unlikely old tale then perhaps the nails were left over from building work associated with the timber-and-earth castle that had been built by the Conyers family.

Every area seems to have its own version of a mischievous, impish demon and in the Chester-le-Street district there are references to a 'brag' at Pelton, Portobello and Picktree. It is thought that the word *brag* may come from an old word *barguest* or *barghaist*, and an alternative name was 'boggle', which could be applied to any ghostly apparition.

Certainly there are regular reports during the nineteenth century of these tiny roguish creatures. At Portobello the brag always appeared in the form of an ass, and whoever mounted it was carried off at speed before being launched into a bog or goose bush. The impish beast then made off 'nickering' or laughing mischievously. Sir Cuthbert Sharp, a nineteenth-century historian from Hartlepool, reported on the alleged behaviour of the Picktree Brag, which appeared in the form of a calf and again dispatched would-be riders into the nearest pond.

Europe's longest pedestrian escalator runs under the Tyne between Jarrow on the south bank and Willington Quay on the opposite side. Construction work began in June 1947 and engineers were faced not only with extremely variable ground conditions but also with the abandoned workings of the old Jarrow and Howdon collieries. Underground workers faced extremely hazardous conditions and by January 1949 miners driving the 12ft-diameter tunnel realised that rock cover above the tunnel was non-existent. Only gravel and silt separated them from the bottom of the river channel and, as the situation worsened, on 2 February 1949, escaping air caused a crater 12ft deep and 40ft wide in the bed of the river. A foaming ring of white water appeared on the surface and the emergency was made worse by a fire in the compressor house. The crater in the river bed was plugged with material dropped from hopper barges and further problems had to be overcome before construction work could be completed. The pedestrian and cyclist tunnels, which are lined with cast-iron segments, were opened by the Minister of Transport, Rt Hon. Alfred Barnes, MP, on 24 July 1951. It is 200ft long and has a vertical rise of 85ft.

For many years the George Hotel at Piercebridge, near Darlington, housed a grandfather clock that has been celebrated in a well-known song. The clock was made by Darlington-based craftsman James Thompson during the early nineteenth century and the ballad featured Mr Christopher Charge, one-time landlord of the George Hotel. Later in life he returned to live at the hotel on the banks of the Tees and brought with him his favourite old clock. When he was confined to bed, the grandfather clock was brought into his room and, as his condition deteriorated, Christopher would point to the clock when it needed

A view of the George Hotel, Piercebridge, home of the legendary grandfather clock.

rewinding. Shortly after his death the clock stopped and all efforts to restart it were unsuccessful. Some time later an American, Henry Clay Work, heard details of the clock's links with Christopher Charge and composed the ballad 'My Grandfather's Clock' with the familiar lines:

> My Grandfather's clock was too large for the shelf
> So it stood ninety years on the floor.
> It was taller by half than the man himself
> Though it weighed not a penny weight more.
> It was bought on the morn of the day that he was born
> And was always his treasure and pride,
> But it stopped short
> Never to go again
> When the old man died.

In these days of instant transworld communications, it is intriguing to recall small-scale operations in remoter rural areas. During the mid-twentieth century key figures in the scattered Upper Teesdale community of Forest in Teesdale were sisters Ailie and Dorothy Redfearn, who ran the local post office and also operated the telephone exchange. They shared this crucial role for thirty-two years. When the exchange became the last in the region to switch to automatic operations in 1969, there were just thirty-nine subscribers. Manning the switchboard throughout the day and long into the night meant that they were unable to take holidays together or jointly attend worship at the nearby Ebenezer Chapel, but their devotion to duty was rightly acknowledged with the award, to both sisters, of the British Empire Medal.

6 Puzzles in Stone & Turf

T hey come in all manner of shapes and sizes. Sometimes they are in their natural form, in other instances they have been shaped by the hand of man; and each one highlights a story about its origins or an important person or event.

The oldest stone feature in the area must be the stump of a fossilised tree that is built into the south wall of the churchyard overlooking Stanhope marketplace. An information plate explains that the tree is some 250 million years old and originally grew in a forest of the Middle Carboniferous Period near Edmundbyers Cross, which is now about 1,350ft above sea level. As its vegetable matter decayed, this was replaced by sand, which has formed a perfect cast in hard ganister. The roots show their characteristic form. The tree was brought to Stanhope and erected at this location in 1962 by Mr H.O. Beaston.

Erratics (glacial boulders) can be found in many parts of our countryside. Brought down from the Pennine Range during the Ice Age, some have been arranged in neat rows during farming work (as along the footpaths south of the Tees between Barnard Castle and Eggleston Abbey), while others have been singled out for display purposes. A prominent grey boulder at the centre of Sadberge village green has a brass inscription that states: 'This stone was placed here to commemorate the jubilee of Victoria, Queen of the United Kingdom, Empress of India and Countess of Sadberge, June 20 1887. It was found 12 feet below the surface in making the reservoir. It had been detached from the rock in the west and deposited by a glacier.'

Another large boulder in Hartburn village sheds light on important aspects of the area's history. Located close to the roadside fence outside the brick-built church in this suburb of Stockton-on-Tees, it was found near the beck, where it was used to beat flax, and it now displays a plaque with the inscription: 'This stone was erected to commemorate the completion of the 60 year reign of Queen Victoria. . . . It was found near the village of Hartburn and was used to beat flax on in former days.' An additional plaque at the base of the stone links the village with the first President of the United States, George Washington. It explains that William de Hertbourne (Hartburn), local lord of the manor, left Hartburn village in 1183 and set up home at Washington in County Durham. His name was changed to William de Wessyngton and one of his direct descendants was the first President of the United States, George Washington. Exactly 800 years later a

Two fossilised trees found in a quarry between Stanhope and Edmundbyers.
One is now in Stanhope Square.

A boulder on Sadberge village green commemorating the Jubilee of Victoria,
Queen of England, Empress of India and Countess of Sadberge, 20 June 1887.

200-strong party of horsemen repeated the 40-mile journey, taking with them a scroll from the Mayor of Stockton, Councillor Brian Hodgson, to President Reagan.

Bulmer's Stone on Darlington's Northgate originated on Shap Fell, Cumbria. This large square-shaped stone was probably named after William Bulmer, who stood on it to read the news (or after the Bulmer family, who owned property in Northgate). The stone may also have been used for beating yarn when Darlington had a flourishing linen industry; until the construction of the town's Technical College the roadside behind the stone was lined with weavers' cottages.

Another fascinating stone, this time with a ring attached, is located outside Darlington's public library in Crown Street. A plaque on the stone states:

This stone, originally in possession of Mr W.T. Stead when resident at Grainey Hill and to which he tethered his dogs and pony, is probably the only monument in granite to his memory in Darlington. The boulder is a fitting symbol of his indomitable courage and strength of character and may keep green the memory of one of England's greatest men. His body perished on the *Titanic* when she sank April 15th 1912. His Spirit Still Lives.

Bulmer's Stone, a glacial erratic, outside cottages on Northgate, Darlington.

A stone located outside Darlington library in memory of Mr W.T. Stead.

The headless statue of 'Albert the Good' in Wharton Park near Durham railway station.

Mystery surrounds an ancient monument some 3 miles south-east of St Helen Auckland. Located in a field beside the Roman road from York to Corbridge (Dere Street), it is known as Legs Cross and consists of a roughly worked shaft (with Saxon Knotwork still visible on one side) supported by a large base resting on a flat stone that shows signs of Roman tool marks and may be part of a Roman milestone. One of the more likely explanations of the name Legs Cross is the suggestion that LEG (legion) was once carved on the stone.

Roadside stonework on Bishopton Lane at Stockton has an even more plaintive and yet intriguing symbol. A block at the top of a flight of steps shows a carving of a simple shovel and is said to have been a humble memorial to one of the workforce who was fatally injured during construction of the underpass below the railway.

A headless statue in Wharton Park near Durham railway station poses any number of unanswerable questions. The stone base displays the inscription 'Albert the Good' and the opposite side is also inscribed. It seems that the base and a nearby oak tree were installed during 1863 by William Lloyd Wharton, chairman of the North Eastern Railway Company, who lived at the neighbouring Dryburn Hall. The inscription explains that the tree was planted to commemorate the marriage of Prince Albert Edward to Princess Alexandra of Denmark on 10 March 1863. Albert Edward was Queen Victoria's eldest son and became King Edward VII on her death in 1901.

Confusion arises because of the fact that it was Victoria's husband, Prince Albert, who was widely known as 'Albert the Good' and it therefore seems that the two tablets on the base of the statue are not referring to the same Albert. During 1862 plans were laid to erect a memorial to Prince Albert within Durham City, but insufficient funds were raised. The headless statue is holding an orb and this seems to indicate a royal figure, so ruling out a Prince Consort or Prince of Wales. The origins of the stone also pose several questions. The likelihood is that it was fashioned during the Victorian period by a sculptor named Gibson and located at another site in the area before being moved to this position, but clear answers may well remain unattainable.

There is more certainty about the statues and carvings of goats that appear around Gateshead. The name Gateshead originally referred to a headland or hill on which goats roamed at Felling and Windy Nook. An inn at the top of Bottle Bank was renamed Goat Inn in about 1650 and a golden goat from the old inn was displayed in Saltwell Park Museum before finding a home in the Shipley Art Gallery on Prince Consort Road. Carvings and statues of goats appear on a number of buildings around the town, including Gateshead town hall and the old Youth Industries Workshop, Public Baths and Laundries building.

The Durham coastline has seen constant changes and the foreshore at Hartlepool is the location of an amazing submerged forest. Stretching for about 400yd to the north and south of Newburn Bridge, it has been designated as a Site of Special Scientific Interest. Thousands of years ago this area had a totally different appearance, with a covering of trees and peat bog. About 8000 BC there was a land bridge linking Britain with the rest of Europe and much of the modern North Sea was low-level fenland. During 1971 a Neolithic male skeleton was uncovered from the site and experts estimate that the man had been between 25 and 35 years old when he was laid on the peat bed in a crouching position on his right side. A small collection of flint flakes had been placed close to his elbow and there was evidence that the body had been covered with branches and twigs of birch.

Sea-defence work allowed close study of the forest during 1990, 1995 and 2002 and this resulted in identification of lines of wooden stakes and worked flints. Erosion of surface peat in 1984 exposed over 2yd of wattle hurdling and after removal and conservation by Durham University these were radiocarbon dated to 3600 BC and identified as part of a fish trap.

A curious relic from modern times is beached on a sandbank close to South Hylton on the River Wear. The *Cretehawser* was one of several concrete vessels that were built by the Wear Concrete Building Company in a yard near Hylton Colliery. Measuring 20ft in length, it was ordered by the Admiralty and completed in 1919. During 1936 it was dismantled and then beached on the sand bank. Other concrete vessels built at the yard include the *Creterope* and the *Cratecable*, which sank after colliding with Yarmouth pier. It was refloated, only to be wrecked three months later after a collision off Whitburn with a trawler called *Lord Cecil*.

Elements of mystery surround four curious ponds on the north side of the A167 near Croft on Tees. Known as Hell's Kettles, they are reported to have been formed on Christmas Day 1179 when the ground rose to a considerable height and remained in that state all day before falling with an enormous crash when darkness fell. Local folk feared that the end of the world was nigh and down the years an amount of folklore grew up around the ponds. Suggestions that they were bottomless were dismissed when the deepest was found to be less than 20ft deep and, although numerous suggestions were put forward about their formation, the most popular theory is that this dramatic movement of the earth's crust was caused by a build-up of gases in the magnesium limestone deposits.

7 Spa Crazy

Close study of historical trends can teach us many lessons – not least the fact that fashions (whether in dress or social activities) – come round at regular intervals. During the early nineteenth century the current fad was for 'taking the waters' and in some places spas continued to attract visitors during the Edwardian era, until the First World War brought any amount of social change. Today an increasing number of hotels and health resorts are advertising spa facilities, though accommodation and domestic arrangements are rather more luxurious.

Some locations were revolutionised during the late eighteenth century by the development of spa buildings, and the arrival of railways, just a few years later, brought increased numbers of visitors. There is little information about Middleton One Row before the end of the eighteenth century, but a chance discovery by workmen during 1789 soon led to dramatic changes. Labourers working for William Henry Lambton were prospecting for coal on his estate at Dinsdale and 'had bored to a depth of 72 feet', chiefly through what they called red rock (Triassic sandstone) and whinstone, when 'the spring burst forth, accompanied with a tremendous smoke and sulphurous stench, so that they were obliged to relinquish their operations in that place during several weeks'.

A similar spring had been operating a few miles away at Croft since the late seventeenth century and its medicinal properties were well known. By 1797 the spring water at Dinsdale had become popular for drinking and bathing, so a cold bath was constructed. This was soon followed by a warm bath and suite of dressing rooms. By 1824 a new baths complex had been completed and properties in nearby Middleton One Row were developed to accommodate visitors.

The opening of the rail link between Stockton and Darlington in 1825 brought an increased number of visitors to the spa and Lord Durham, William Lambton's son, built a large hotel on the summit of the high river bank above the bath house. Designed by Bonomi and completed at a cost of about £30,000, it included over seventy well-furnished apartments and stabling facilities, which made it a suitable venue for balls and other social gatherings during the summer months.

Middleton One Row soon boasted a whole range of tradespeople, an efficient postal service and a free lending library, but Dinsdale Spa Hotel enjoyed fairly short-lived prosperity and during the 1850s it became a centre for a limited number of the higher and middle classes whose state of mind required seclusion and medical treatment.

Dinsdale Spa Hotel near Middleton One Row.

Looking upstream from Middleton One Row towards the spa buildings and the hotel.

A view across the village green at Middleton One Row,
with Devonport Hotel on the right-hand side.

St Lawrence's Church, Middleton One Row.

Taking the waters at Gainford spa.

A similar but smaller-scale development took place further upstream on the banks of the Tees in Gainford. During the late eighteenth century a spa was set up at a location about a quarter of a mile west of the village and, as its popularity increased, a fountain and standpipe were installed. Guest houses were constructed around the village green in order to accommodate visitors to the health-giving spa waters and Gainford became a popular place of retirement for people from the Darlington area. Ambitious plans were made to pipe water from the fountainhead to a position on the green, but these never materialised. The spa itself continued in use until the outbreak of the First World War, but in more recent years the fontlike basin that capped the sulphurous spring water was badly vandalised. During the year 2002 a replacement basin and fittings were installed and the word is that, in small doses, the cold, clear, strong-smelling waters are still good for one's health!

There are few signs of the spa that was located in woodland upstream from Barnard Castle, but further north at Shotley Bridge there are several reminders of the town's health-giving waters. During the late 1830s Dr Augustus Granville, a naval surgeon, completed a tour of spas throughout England and found Shotley Bridge Spa 'well situated nearly in the centre of an ornamental garden about a mile below the village'. He explained that 'the water, which is limpid and perfectly colourless, rises in a horizontal stream, through a spout in an upright stone which covers the well', and after careful analysis suggested that 'the Shotley Bridge Spa water may be made instrumental in the recovery of many disorders which no other water in the country can cure. The water differs in its composition from all the others I have examined in my recent tour.' The development of spa facilities was carried out by a Quaker, Jonathan Richardson, from 1837 and the town's location between Durham and Newcastle (as well as just 12 miles from Hexham) brought an influx of visitors including Charles Dickens (during 1839). Large detached houses, some with an Alpine appearance appropriate to the wooded and hilly landscape, were built along Cutler's Hall Road and Snow's Green Road at the peak of the spa's popularity.

The 58-acre Saltwell Park at Gateshead was landscaped for public use in 1877 and at the centre of the ornamental gardens was a distinctive mansion known as Saltwell Towers. The name of the park was derived from a salt well that was renowned for its healthy properties.

Several northern seaside resorts had the added attraction of spa waters, but one of the most curious was located on the sands at Hartlepool. No doubt the presence of this bubbling spring fascinated the growing number of holiday-makers who combined a visit to this shore-based curiosity with games of whist or searches for human remains among nearby sand dunes. The exact position of the spring has caused an amount of debate, but the usual setting is said to have been on the north side of the Sandwell Gate, where fresh water seeped from higher ground and flowed on top of heavier salt water. During the spa's peak of popularity in the late eighteenth century a well was constructed on the fish sands in order to draw off the waters. By the time of Dr Augustus Granville's

The salt well at Saltwell Park at Gateshead.

visit in 1839 the spa was no longer operating, but during the late 1990s high tides exposed a well head. Possible links with the spa were dismissed when it was established that it served a Victorian public house, the Freemasons Arms, which was built in the 1850s and probably demolished in the 1930s.

Butterby, near Durham City, had three mineral springs. One was located in the bed of the River Wear and contained large amounts of iron and common salt, but the other two land-based spas attracted considerable interest in the early 1800s. Dr Granville reported that these were sited in 'a most romantic dell, the sides of which are deep, and shadowed by overhanging wood'. The first spring was known as the 'Sweet Well', because it was tasteless apart from a small amount of carbonate of lime. Further down the dell a second spring contained an amount of sulphur, but according to Dr Granville's report the presence of muriate of soda, lime and magnesia prevented it from tasting too disagreeable.

It was the same sort of sulphur spa at Axwell Park to the west of Gateshead, where Dr Granville noted that the water was 'pleasant to the taste and giving out a few bubbles of free gas'.

8 Monster Mania

Each area has its own unique set of monster legends, but in each case the central strand is usually the same. More often than not a brave local knight confronts and then dispatches the loathsome serpent that had terrorised the neighbourhood with demands for supplies of food and slaves.

Sockburn nestles at the southern end of a meandering loop in the Tees some 7 miles south-east of Darlington. With a ruined medieval chapel, Tudor-style Victorian hall and deserted village site, it makes an ideal setting for a fascinating serpent saga. Variously described in early documents as 'a dragon or fiery, flying serpent', this dreaded monster was said to have a scent 'so strong that no person was able to abide it', and it continued to terrorise the neighbourhood until the appearance of a brave young knight, John Conyers. Conyers confronted the monster, but an old manuscript informs us that 'before he did enterprise it (having but one child) he went to the church in complete armour and offered

The ruins of All Saints' Church, Sockburn.

All Saints' Church, Sockburn.

up his son to the Holy Ghost'. The loathsome worm was duly vanquished, and its burial place is said to be under a limestone boulder in an adjacent field at Graystone.

John Conyers's reward for ridding the area of this menacing beast was said to have been ownership of the Sockburn estates, and among the collection of pre-Norman and medieval relics in the restored chapel is an effigy of a cross-legged warrior. He is wearing chain mail and a flowing surcoat, his right hand is grasping the hilt of his sheathed sword and at his feet a lion is fighting a dragon. It is tempting to believe that the effigy represents John Conyers, slayer of the Sockburn worm, or one of his immediate descendants.

For those looking for an explanation of the origins of the legend, there is plenty of evidence of Viking-age sculptures within the collection at the chapel, and it is known that the Conyers family moved to Sockburn from Bishopton (near Stockton-on-Tees) after organising resistance to Scottish raiders. Whether a member of the Conyers family was rewarded for putting paid to a Viking or

The restored chapel at All Saints' Church, Sockburn.

Sockburn Hall, close to the site of the deserted village and ruined church.

Scottish chieftain will never be known, but an interesting ceremony linking the bishops of Durham with Sockburn takes place on Croft Bridge to mark the arrival of a new bishop. Proceedings involve the presentation of the Conyers falchion (a medieval broadsword) to the bishop by the Lords of the Manor of Sockburn. The ceremony most recently took place on 4 July 2003, when the new bishop of Durham, Dr Tom Wright, was presented with the falchion by the area dean, the Revd John Dobson.

The village of Brancepeth, which spreads on the north and south sides of the A690 between Willington and Durham, is probably best known for its castle and church. An early medieval fortress on the site was home to the powerful Neville family, who lost it after their involvement in the 1569 rebellion of northern barons. After several owners, it was purchased by William Russell, a banker and coal owner from Sunderland, in 1796 and it was his son, Matthew, who spent tens of thousands of pounds from 1819 creating the dramatic spectacle that we see today. Distant views from the south are impressive, but closer inspection of the huge mock Norman gatehouse and bulging round towers reveals an almost theatrical appearance. Most of the stonework on walls around the central courtyard also dates from the 1820s, with only portions remaining of earlier medieval buildings.

Close at hand, across grassy lawns, the church of St Brandon has recently been innovatively restored after a destructive fire had gutted the interior in the late 1990s.

The village name originated from another local monster legend involving a fearsome beast, the Brawn, and its peth (path) from a nearby lair down to the

Brancepeth Castle (with its name derived from Brawn's peth)

River Wear. The Brawn's den lies about 1½ miles north-west of Brancepeth, but archaeologists have identified nothing more sinister than an Iron Age or Roman British settlement. (It is also the name for a public house at the western end of Brandon.) Some 6 miles away to the south-east, near Ferryhill, a farm has a fragment of inscribed stone built into the coping of its roadside wall. Lettering on the stone states: 'The large stone just above, part of Cleves Cross, marks the site where by tradition the Brawn of Brancepeth was killed by Roger de Fery about the year 1200.'

The stone near Ferryhill that marks the spot where the Brawn of Brancepeth was killed.

The area's best-known monster legend features the Lambton worm. According to this folk tale, the river-based serpent was fished out of the Wear by a young member of the Lambton family on a Sunday morning when he should have been attending church. Alarmed by his unexpected catch, the lad is said to have thrown the snake into a nearby well, where it soon grew to a great size and began to terrorise the neighbourhood from its lair on Penshaw Hill. Some time later the young Lambton heir returned from the Crusades and consulted a wise woman about tactics for overcoming the monster. He was advised that his only hope of success was to protect himself with armour studded with razor blades and then attack the beast on its rock in midstream, where the current would wash away its severed parts, thus avoiding the danger of their being rejoined. For his part, Lambton had to kill the next living creature that he came across, 'or the lords of Lambton would not die in their beds for nine generations'.

The monstrous serpent was safely dispatched, but, in celebrating his son's success, the old father forgot to unleash a favourite hound as the promised sacrifice and ran to congratulate his young knight. The hound was duly sacrificed, but too late, and for the next nine generations, so it is said, no Lambton died in his bed.

Penshaw Hill (and monument), the legendary lair of the Lambton worm.

The story of the
Hartlepool monkey.

In more recent times Hartlepool has become well known for its monkey legend. Set in the early nineteenth century, when there was widespread fear of an invasion by Napoleonic forces, a raft was washed ashore during stormy weather. Although it was suggested by wiser counsel that the sole occupant of the raft was a monkey, the consensus among the crowd of onlookers was that it must be a French spy. A mock trial was arranged and when the stranger was subjected to questioning its babbling response was taken as proof of its guilt. The unfortunate castaway was condemned to die for treason and a gibbet was set up on the Fish Sands.

Similar stories are told around parts of Britain, including Cornwall and at Boddam in Aberdeenshire, where local wreckers lured a ship on to the rocks. The ship's monkey was the only survivor, but it was promptly hanged by the wrecking party so that they could claim the cargo.

The Hartlepool episode was popularised during the 1950s by a north-east entertainer, Ned Corvan, who wrote a song called 'The Fishermen Hung the Monkey O'. It was probably based on a song from Tyneside called 'The Baboon', which was published in 1827 and described the pursuit of a baboon, dressed in uniform, by local pitmen. It had escaped from a travelling menagerie, but local pitmen believed it was a French spy. Ned Corvan performed the song for the first time at Dock Street Music Hall in Hartlepool and the town was very quickly recognised as the setting for the monkey legend. One of the local rugby teams, Hartlepool Rovers, focused attention on the legend by hanging a stuffed monkey from the crossbar before each match during the 1890s. They even took it on tour with the team, where the story attracted coverage from national newspapers.

Stories of monsters and 'monkeys' have their roots in the realms of distant folklore, spiced with elements of truth, and they often receive limited serious consideration. Yet in recent years there have been persistent reported sightings of exotic creatures in the north-east. The most enduring claims focus on the so-called Durham puma. These wily animals were kept as pets and released into the wild after the Dangerous Wild Animals Act of 1976 forced owners to buy a licence for their wild cats. The first recorded sighting of a puma was in August 1986 and droppings found several years ago confirmed their existence, though so far they have all eluded capture.

Another type of cat that is to be found in rural parts is the lynx, which was once native to this country and is thought to have been wiped out in Roman times. However, it is likely that some survived in isolated pockets and have managed to prosper away from human eyes. Experts also estimate that there could be as many as twenty-five wild boar on the loose in County Durham alone.

The statue of the Hartlepool monkey in Hartlepool marina.

They can grow to 6ft in length, weighing in at more than 20 stone and with a speed of 30mph, but, despite their 5in tusks and incredible bulk, boar are shy creatures. Two breeding populations exist in Sussex and Dorset and reports suggest that numbers could reach almost 3,500 by 2012. After more than 300 years of extinction in the wild in Britain, boars could become a common sight once again as they roam freely in the countryside.

The most recent sightings of a mystery beast were reported in December 2003 when a woman motorist claimed to have seen 'a big ferret-like creature' on moors between Rookhope and Ireshopeburn in Weardale. A spokesman for 'Beastwatch' suggested that the animal was probably a wolverine, a relative of the skunk that can grow up to 18in tall and is powerfully built, with sharp teeth and a bushy tail.

Reports of strange creatures have reached such a pitch that since 1985 Durham police have detailed a wildlife officer to investigate around 400 sightings of unusual animals. He has been able to provide an explanation for each one, although in about sixty cases it did turn out that there was a creature that was not meant to be there. Perhaps he is very close to the truth when he suggests that 'we genuinely want something to be different in our lives . . . we want to be excited, to take us away from our boring, everyday lives'; but who knows – there might just be a monstrous beast lurking out there somewhere.

9 Sports & Customs

In the world of sport, it is strange to see how grand events and splendid occasions often come to an abrupt end and slip away from recent memory, while some obscure sports continue as years roll by.

Race week at Durham City attracted visitors from a wide area of north-east England and a whole range of social events was staged to provide maximum enjoyment for race-goers. Theatrical productions, dinners, balls and the rather less edifying 'mains of cocks' created an atmosphere of excitement and conviviality in support of the series of races. It is not known when racing first began at Durham, but by 1613 it was well established on Woodham Moor. Inevitably there were changing fortunes for racecourses and by 1835 many meetings were suffering from falling attendances and a general decline in the level of interest, but the last day of Durham's race week coincided with market day, a cattle fair and the hiring of household servants. Contemporary reports

An event taking place on Durham City racecourse.

describe lots of drinking, plenty of shows and, as the day wore on, a fight or two. An evening's entertainment at the theatre attracted large numbers, while others converged on Mr Ralph Salkeld's pit (for cock fighting) at the Waterloo Inn, where the action began at 9 p.m.

By the mid-1830s racing had moved to the riverside course, where it continued, with brief absences, for over forty years. Located within the bend of the River Wear, the course was rather cramped for riders and spectators alike, and the support and influence of north-country families such as the Lambtons, Vyners and Shaftos was vital in keeping the course open. The end of racing at Durham came in July 1887 after a two-day meeting when university authorities decided not to renew the lease of the racecourse ground.

Blaydon Races were immortalised in a song that tells of crowds making their way along the Scotswood Road to the old course, which was located on an area of land close to the confluence of the Tyne and Derwent. The races were last held in 1916 and a power station was then built on the site.

The north-east is widely known as the hotbed of soccer, but a rather different ball game, with origins in the early medieval period, attracts considerable attention to Sedgefield on Shrove Tuesday. It is said to have originated as early as 1072 and may have been regarded as entertainment before the fasting of Lent. Originally it was a contest between artisans and farmworkers and at the heart of the action was a small leather ball, made in secret by a saddler in Darlington. Local publicans used to supply the ball and start the game, but proceedings now get under way

A view of the centre of Sedgefield in 1913.

The millennium stone tablet celebrating Sedgefield's Shrove Tuesday football game.

The Shrove Tuesday football game in progress.

Chester-le-Street Shrove Tuesday football game.

when a local resident, or previous exponent of the game, passes the all-important ball through the bull ring at the northern end of the green. As the nearby parish church clock shows 1 p.m. the starter calls 'Alley off' as he hurls the ball into the expectant throng. Alleying places or goals are located about a quarter of a mile apart, but the ball is kicked, carried and thrown all around the township and into every local public house before reaching a goal. If the ball has not been alleyed by 6 o'clock in the evening, it becomes the property of the sexton.

A similar contest used to take place at Chester-le-Street, where a ball was dropped from the window of a local pub to start the action, but this general free-for-all was ended in 1932. Another local game that has fallen out of favour is knurr and spell, a poor man's golf that used to be played in the area.

A rather more complicated ball game takes place at Ushaw College, a few miles west of Durham City. The game of 'cat' is believed to have originated at Douai, in France, before Roman Catholic authorities established the seminary at Ushaw, and a comprehensive rulebook has been regularly updated in more recent years. There are elements of rounders, squash and perhaps cricket in this fast and furious encounter, which revolves around a tiny hard stuffed ball, rounders bats and a perimeter wall. Reports suggest that the pace of the game has slowed in recent years because participants tend to be former pupils of maturing years!

One of County Durham's most endearing customs takes place at Whitburn, where a 'hot pot' or loving cup is prepared, on request, for weddings at the local parish church. Either bride or groom must have been born in Whitburn and the secret potion is produced in a silver loving cup with two handles; the warm, sweet drink is supposed to guarantee future happiness. Made from a recipe passed down from generation to generation, this secret beverage was originally tasted only by the bride and groom, but nowadays other members of the wedding party are allowed a sip. In the past the loving cup has been taken as far afield as York, but during 2003 it was requested on only one occasion.

Durham Cathedral is linked with a curious custom that has links with the battle of Neville's Cross in 1346. Scottish forces under King David II had reached the north-western outskirts of Durham City before they were met and vanquished by English troops led by the Archbishop of York and the Bishops of Durham and Lincoln. It was a case of English longbows triumphing over Scottish pikemen, and throughout the three-hour battle English troops were given support by a group of monks who sang Mass on top of the cathedral tower. The abbot vowed that, if the English army was victorious, Mass would be sung there on each anniversary of the battle. Each year anthems are sung from the tower on 29 May, but only from three sides. A chorister once fell to his death on the fourth side and authorities will not risk this happening again.

Knurr and spell, a game known as poor man's golf, in progress at Middleton-in-Teesdale.

Pitch for the game of 'cat' at Ushaw College.

Ushaw College near Durham City.

Durham Cathedral, where anthems are sung on the anniversary
of the battle of Neville's Cross.

An unlikely tale suggests that if a person walks nine times round the cross that marks the site of the battle and then puts an ear to the ground, then the sounds of battle may be clearly heard.

A curious coincidence surrounds Grafton House in South Street, Durham. Built in about 1900, this impressive Edwardian townhouse has only ever been lived in by women. It overlooks the River Wear with fine views of the cathedral and was built by a clergyman's widow, Eleanor Charlton. She died in 1908 and left the house to her spinster daughter Beatrice Charlton, who lived there unmarried until her death in 1963. For much of that time she was not alone, as her sister Geraldine Wilkinson, who was widowed in 1932, and Geraldine's daughter came to live with her.

Gwendolyn inherited Grafton House on her aunt's death in 1963 and lived there until her own death in February 2003, when the house was put up for sale.

10 What's in a Name

Place names have any number of origins, but there are times when a logical or rational explanation remains extremely elusive. Often the name gives the flavour of an area, with indications of the type of local landscape or industrial background; at times it can be linked with a prominent local personality from the world of politics, the armed services or sport, and even an important national or local event. Then, of course, there are place names showing strong links with early settlers (during the Anglo-Saxon or Viking periods) – and if all obvious leads draw a blank, then there is always inspired speculation!

Bearpark is located some 3 miles west of Durham City and the name perhaps conjures up images of animals and circuses. In fact, the parish and village of Bearpark derive their name from the medieval manor house and chapel of Beaurepaire, whose Norman French name means 'the beautiful retreat'.

Bearpark Colliery coke ovens.

It represented the largest and probably most important manor house in the ownership of the Priory of Durham. Built for Prior Bertram de Middleton between 1258 and 1274, it was used by successive priors as a rural retreat and monarchs were entertained here during the late fourteenth and early fifteenth centuries. Following closure in 1541, the buildings were neglected and further damage occurred during the English Civil War of the 1640s, but it is still possible to trace the layout of rooms among the ruins of this fascinating location.

Parts of Bearpark Hall Farm date from about 1475 and the earliest references to coal mining in the area appear in the mid-fifteenth century. The local colliery opened in 1847 and by 1900 some 1,000 men and boys were employed to work seven seams. It closed in 1984 and pit heaps have since been landscaped.

Another location with possible French origins is Pity Me. This is a plaintive sort of name in modern times, but the most likely theory is that it is a corruption of *petit mer* – a little lake or pond that used to be seen in the village. Another

A snow scene on Front Street, Pity Me, 1 February 1947. The town's name is probably derived from the French words *petit mer*, meaning small lake.

suggestion for this area, close to Durham City's northern fringe, is 'pitty mea' meaning an uneven meadow.

Byshottles represents an old, long-disused name for Brandon. This is possibly rooted in Anglo-Saxon vocabulary, *scytels* meaning a bolt or bar and *scaden* meaning to divide. Its origins may be linked with either a town latrine or a lock-up. Other locations with possible links to Old English vocabulary include Hett, which is located some 5 miles south of Durham City to the east of the A167. This curiously named little village, with a scattering of cottages and modern houses around a wide green, may have the meaning of 'heath moor' or possibly 'hat', relating to features on surrounding slopes. Kyo could be derived from an Old English term meaning 'cow hill', while Wham is linked with the Old English *hwamme* meaning corner, and Witherwack's Old English connections could include *wether*, a reference to sheep, or possibly an Old Norse word for willow.

Sadberge near Darlington is said to be the only place in the country with this name, which may derive from *Sac Beorth* meaning the court on the hill. This gives an indication of the earlier importance of this shrunken village, which used to be located at the centre of the Wapentake of Sadberge. During the medieval period it had its own sheriff, coroner and other civil officers, and an assize court, commissioned by the Bishop of Durham, sat here until the mid-fifteenth century, when it was moved to Durham. There were also a castle, court house and jail (with the office of jailer continuing until 1862).

Some names have no obvious origins and encourage a range of speculative explanations. Toronto, Quaking Houses and Philadelphia fall into this category, along with Deaf Hill, an alternative name for Trimdon Station, while California is said to be linked with a local farmer's sarcastic term for a particularly infertile or remote field. On the other hand, Fatfield, essentially a nineteenth-century coal-mining settlement, could have originated from a farmer's reference to a really fertile area. Dragonville developed during the nineteenth century and probably took its name from the George and Dragon public house.

Important military victories are reflected in place names such as Quebec, which celebrates General Wolfe's victory over French forces in 1757; Inkerman, an important Crimean War success against Russian troops; and Vigo, situated on Birtley's southern fringe, which was developed in the eighteenth century after British forces captured the Spanish seaport of this name in 1719.

Most intriguing of all, however, must be No Place, which actually does exist close to the A693 near Beamish Village. This tiny almost anonymous settlement originated as a group of four or five cottages close to the Robin Hood public house (on the approach to Cooperative Villas from the east) and it was so called because this handful of properties was in the 'no man's land' between the district councils of Stanley on the western side and Chester-le-Street to the east.

Inn signs are also the source of much debate, with animals and fish often featuring in these improbable tales. Dancing bears are fairly unusual, but there

No Place Nobblers Prize Jazz Band, photographed at Wallsend Carnival.

Ralph William Robinson wearing the No Place Nobblers outfit for the last time before giving it to the Beamish Museum.

Shields' corner shop, No Place.

is probably only one Balancing Eel in the entire country and it is to be found at South Shields. It shows a sailor with an eel balanced on his nose, and, when we look for an explanation, there is not a theatrical link, as might have been expected, but rather an illustration of a line from a poem about an old man who was intent on proving that his eyesight and sense of balance were as steady as ever . . . and so he balanced an eel on the end of his nose.

11 Out of Print

L ocal newspapers not only report on events of national and international importance, but also turn the spotlight on unusual or lesser-known events and personalities.

On a sporting theme, there was a report of a would-be prize fight at Stockton in the spring of 1873. A location near the cemetery on Oxbridge Lane had been chosen for the prize fight between the South Stockton and Stockton 'Champions', who were 'well known in select circles . . . Several hundred men gathered together to witness proceedings but unfortunately for the gratification of their appetite the whole of the arrangements were known to the police and Supt Booth had provided a detachment to attend the Sabbath Day entertainment, thus frustrating the intentions of the combatants . . .'.

Promoters, boxers and fighters had a rather more successful outing on Friday 13 March 1885, when the championship of the north was held near Barnard Castle. The prize fight between Johnnie Robinson of Shields and Tom Johnson of Sunderland lasted forty-three minutes, during which they fought twenty-nine rounds before Johnson's second 'threw up the sponge . . . The men then shook hands and with their backers got quietly away.'

In 1888 it was not prize fighting but the new craze of football that saw several Stockton men brought before the court. They were charged with street obstruction on 6 February after PC Garbutt had found them in Chalk Street kicking a bladder about. Each man was ordered to pay 3s inclusive of costs.

A spectacular event took place on Victoria Bridge, between Stockton and Thornaby-on-Tees, on the afternoon of 20 January 1890. Local newspapers reported that Tommy Burns, a professional swimmer, accomplished the daring feat of jumping off the Victoria Bridge at the prearranged time of 3.55 p.m.

Burns, accompanied by Mr Cuthbert Gardner of the Star Music Hall, drove on to the bridge in a cab, simply attired in a scarlet bathing suit. Burns climbed the parapet of the bridge and took his leap from a ledge about 24 feet above high water level. The tide was at its highest at the time. On reaching the water Burns turned over on his back and then sank but immediately regained the surface and after throwing a somersault and shaking himself he commenced to swim down stream with a hand over hand stroke. The water was, however, too cold for a protracted stay and when he reached Rudd's wharf the swimmer scrambled into a boat and was rowed ashore, afterwards being conveyed to his hotel in a cab.

Victoria Bridge, where Tommy Burns performed his daring stunt on 20 January 1890.

Just a few months earlier the local press had carried reports of a 'Perilous Adventure' by a Mr Dorie, who made a balloon ascent from the Belle Vue Grounds at Stockton before 'exhibiting one of his daring parachute descents through two miles of space'.

For those who wanted indoor entertainment, the Grand Theatre, Stockton, offered wonderful value at the end of December 1897. Artistes included 'The Ross Combination' in 'Mr Maloney's Troubles', assisted by the Marvellous Midgets; Miss Mabel Comley, seriocomic and low-comedy artiste; Allen McAshell, conjuror and funny patterer; Sister Powers, skirt, step and skipping-rope dancer; Ashley and Beach, negro comedians; Will Saunders, comedian and leg mania artiste; Queenie Palmer, serio and ballad vocalist; Dueman, conjuror and electrician; Harry Dashwood, character comedian and actor vocalist; and James Curran, from London, star comedian and parody king.

Weather conditions make the headlines from time to time and they must have been a major talking point during the 1870s. Press reports in July 1874 gave details of a whirlwind and thunderstorm at Middleton One Row, first observed in one of Mr Emmerson's turnip fields, traversing down the field and across the River Tees. On reaching the woods near the spa baths, the whirlwind swept the gravel and sand off the walks up into the air to a considerable height above the treetops, tearing off their leaves and branches and carrying them over the houses in the village of Middleton One Row. On its way to the village, the whirlwind

The Grand Theatre, Stockton, which was later restyled as the Plaza Cinema.

again crossed the river, sucking the water up into the air and scattering it in all directions. Two anglers were greatly frightened.

A destructive thunderstorm raged through Teesdale on 12 May 1878 leaving several trees uprooted and abutments on a railway bridge severely damaged, but even this was probably eclipsed by the thunderbolt that ripped into a house on Surbiton Road at Stockton on 10 June 1987.

Other extremes of weather made news headlines and in December 1878 the County Durham area saw its coldest weather for years. The River Tees froze over above Stockton Bridge and 'on Saturday 14 December Billingham Bottoms were visited by about 3,000 people and, as a charge of 3d per head was made, the owner of the flooded land made a handsome profit'.

Visits by wild animals also brought headlines. On 20 December 1875 Mrs Edmunds's (later Wombwell's) Windsor Castle menagerie of wild beasts arrived in Stockton on a Saturday morning and proceeded throughout the town prior to taking up position in the marketplace. The splendid stud of elephants, camels, dromedaries and horses attracted immense crowds of followers and in the afternoon and evening the great zoological display was patronised by crowded and delighted audiences. 'This is unquestionably the best collection that has been exhibited in the district for some time. It proceeds to Greatham on Monday.'

A rather unwelcome visitor from the animal world featured in reports during November 1888: 'A very sensational incident has just occurred at Bishop Auckland. About twenty minutes to ten o'clock on Sunday night a married woman named Mary Foster residing with her husband at 35 South Terrace went upstairs where two children were sleeping in a bed and as she opened the bedroom door she observed a fox spring up in one corner of the bed in which the children were sleeping. She gave an alarm. Reynard ran downstairs and was ultimately killed by Mr Foster.'

Fish farms are a feature of many rural areas, and in April 1874 a Stockton man was breeding salmon in downtown Stockton.

Mr Jeremiah Wilson of Oxford Street, a boilersmith by trade, has again been successful in hatching some thousands of young salmon and it may be here stated that specimens of the result of his labours were objects of much interest at the recent meeting of the Salmon Fishery Board . . . His work took place in a yard attached to his house, where two tanks were lined with slate and covered at the bottom with small stones in which the tiny fish may now be seen darting about. Then, when free from the eggs, they are placed in a large tank and in due course placed in the river to replenish the stock from whence our food supply is procured. This has been a hobby of Mr Wilson for some years.

Attention was focused on Stockton again during March 1892, when a Russian gunboat arrived in the Tees.

Some commotion was caused . . . by the arrival of a detachment of the Russian Imperial Navy who have come to take charge of a new gunboat which is being fitted out by Messrs R. Craggs & Sons, Shipbuilders. The *Oithana* is a steel screw steamer of 700 tons gross register, built in Aberdeen and is included in Lloyd's List of fast steamers as a 13 knot vessel. Having been purchased by the Russian government, her name will be changed to Yakoub and she is intended for special coastguard service in protection of Russian fisheries in the Japan Sea . . . The alterations have been carried out under the personal supervision of Captain Chinielenski, who will take command of the gunboat. Messrs W. Bennington Sons are supplying rations to the crew during their short stay in Stockton.

During July 1916 an unusual set of stocks made headlines with a report that:

Away from the gaze of the general public has been placed a pair of stocks discovered in Durham Prison. Inquiries amongst the eldest of the citizens show that these stocks were in use about seventy years ago, having previously been removed from the old prison, which was closed nearly a century ago. A noted poacher was the last person to occupy these stocks, which now have been placed within the portals of the prison. Anyone committing an offence and being consigned to prison will have the 'pleasure' of seeing them but probably the keenest archaeologist would hesitate to adopt that method of gratifying the desire to contemplate the relics of the past.

Norton Green, where the 'girl blacksmith' operated
from a forge on the right of the photograph.

Preston Hall, home of *The Diceplayers* by Georges de la Tour.

On a lighter note, a 'Norton girl blacksmith' made headlines in March 1944 when it was reported that this girl welder, riveter and blacksmith's assistant was to broadcast to American, Canadian and British listeners about her working day. The young lady in question was 19-year-old Audrey Samuelson, daughter of the Norton blacksmith, and her story was told in a programme called *From All Over Britain* for the BBC and Pacific Service.

The later months of 1973 brought dramatic reports of the discovery of an important work of art at Stockton. Amazingly, a collection of 149 paintings that had been kept in storage at Preston Hall included a watercolour by Turner, a Lowry picture of early Middlesbrough and most valuable of all, a lost masterpiece, *The Diceplayers* by Georges de la Tour (1593–1652).

12 Things Ain't What They Used To Be

Buildings are fascinating, aren't they? Even recent properties are well worth a closer look in order to identify materials, styles of architecture, alterations and reason for construction. Older buildings may well hold more interest, and, although many fine properties have disappeared under the demolition expert's hammer, it is surprising how a range of properties can take on a new lease of life with an alternative use.

Many former village schools throughout the country have been converted into comfortable family residences, as at Whorlton near Barnard Castle. Sometimes the school building was adapted as a church, as happened at Hartburn on Stockton's western fringe. The British School in Hartburn village was opened on

Weardale Inn, formerly the Newhouse School at Ireshopeburn.

A stone tablet at the former Newhouse School.

12 January 1877, but the day school vacated the premises in 1911. During the next two years this single-storey red-brick building was converted for use as an Anglican place of worship and dedicated for church use by Bishop H.C.G. Moule of Durham on 24 June 1913. But it is quite a different story at Winston, near Barnard Castle, and Ireshopeburn in upper Weardale. Lead mining in Weardale was at its height during the mid-nineteenth century, and, as workers and their families flocked into local communities, facilities were completed for different members of the family. In 1854 the Newhouse School was built at Ireshopeburn on land given by W.B. Beaumont Esq., MP, at a cost of £1,400. Mr Beaumont, lessee of the Weardale mines, contributed £900, and a further £500 was raised by subscriptions from his agents, miners and villagers 'for the education of children of all religious denominations' (as indicated on a stone tablet in the adjacent car park). School fees for miners' children (totalling 4*d* per week in 1877) were paid by the Lead Company. In recent years the school has closed and the building has become the Weardale Inn.

It is a similar story at Winston, where the former village school building has been converted into a public house, the Bridgewater Arms.

Churches and chapels have also made the transformation from place of worship to private house or business premises. The tiny former Methodist chapel on the Avenue at Fairfield, Stockton-on-Tees, has become a private residence, but the much larger Paradise Row Primitive Methodist church on the town's Church

The Bridgewater Arms at Winston.
The former village school building now houses the inn.

The former Methodist church on
Paradise Row, Stockton-on-Tees.

The former Methodist church at Hartlepool, which is now a nightclub.

The former Brunswick Methodist church,
Stockton-on-Tees, now a carpet shop.

The Sunday school premises of the
former Brunswick Methodist chapel.

The interior of the former Brunswick Methodist church.

Road has served in recent years as a store for doors, windows and wallpapers. The church opened in 1866 and closed for worship in 1945, but above recent shop fittings it is still possible to pick out decorative features such as devils and skeleton dogs from the building's days as a church.

Brunswick Methodist church on Dovecot Street, Stockton-on-Tees, has the date 1823 on a carved stone over the door. The Sunday school premises at the rear were opened during the following year, but both buildings are now used as business premises. While rolls of carpet dominate the interior of Stockton's Brunswick church, it is the sights and sounds of merrymakers that fill West Hartlepool's former Methodist church on Grange Road. This large brick building was built in the early 1870s with a high Corinthian-style portico in stone and still dominates the eastern end of Victoria Road. After standing empty and unused for a number of years, it has found an alternative use as a nightclub with the name Wesley's. Methodism's founding father John Wesley would surely turn in his grave!

Cinemas have regularly made the switch to bingo halls (as at Billingham) or private houses (as at Middleton St George), but some larger premises have seen even more impressive changes of use. When the Daylight Bakery on Bishopton Avenue at Stockton became vacant, it faced an uncertain future. It represented a fine example of late 1930s factory architecture, featuring a central clock tower above an attractive canopied entrance, and the whole frontage was covered in glazed tiles. Tasteful conversion of the building into apartments has retained the original architectural details.

The huge silo of the Baltic Flour Mill has dominated Gateshead's river frontage for more than half a century. Opened in 1950, the set of buildings was operated by Joseph Rank Ltd for the production of flours and animal feed until operations ended in 1982. Most of the buildings were demolished, leaving only the silo as a stolid-looking sentinel facing an uncertain future. A splendidly imaginative scheme saw the silo at the centre of the Gatehead Quays project, along with the Millennium Bridge and adjacent music centre. Its conversion to the Baltic Centre for Contemporary Art as part of this £250 million scheme represents a wonderfully enterprising use for this former industrial building.

A similarly impressive adaptation of a huge structure has taken place in recent years at Bishop Auckland, where the Newton Cap Viaduct spans the River Wear. Built between 1854 and 1857 as part of the Bishop Auckland Branch contract, the viaduct measures 100ft in height (from the riverbed to the rails) and is made up of eleven arches (each one with a span of 60ft). Ten piers measuring 8ft in width and two abutments of 44ft complete this superb engineering feat. A similar viaduct in Durham City still carries the main east-coast line between London and Edinburgh, while a third example is located on the outskirts of Durham at Brasside.

The chief engineer for the North Eastern Railway was Thomas Elliot Harrison; he was a pupil of Robert Stephenson and the pair had worked together

Above: The Baltic Flour Mill from the Millennium Bridge.

Left: The former Baltic Flour Mill with conversion work in progress
to convert the premises to an arts complex.

during 1849 on the High Level Bridge at Newcastle as well as the Berwick on Tweed railway. A special train of twenty-two carriages crossed the viaduct on 1 April 1857 to mark the official opening, and the last train crossed in 1968. It was acquired by Durham County Council in 1972 and two years later it had been converted into a footway as part of the network of country walks.

Increasing congestion on the nearby Newton Cap road bridge prompted plans for alternative river crossings. Suggestions that the viaduct was structurally unsound resulted in a campaign to safeguard its future and further investigations showed that it was in fact well built. A unique conversion of the viaduct from rail to road traffic as part of a £5.85 million road improvement scheme began in 1993. There was a delay in building work when a kestrel's nest was discovered, but the new high-level route opened in 1995 and represented the first conversion scheme of its kind in the United Kingdom.

The Beehive Ballroom stood empty and unused on the Lingfield Point site, off McMullen Road, Darlington, for about fifteen years until redevelopment plans

Newton Cap Viaduct, Bishop Auckland.

were announced in January 2004. During its heyday the premises served as the social club for Paton and Baldwins, who employed more than 4,000 people, and its name was derived from the company's beehive logo. Conversion work is under way in 2004 to create six split-level offices while retaining many original features, including decorative ceilings.

13 Vanished Glories

Redevelopment and regeneration schemes are a regular feature in most of our towns and cities, as outdated and redundant buildings are superseded by state-of-the-art business and commercial premises. County Durham is well known for the construction of complete new towns such as Peterlee and Washington during the second half of the twentieth century, but a look at earlier days highlights a whole collection of once-thriving settlements that have disappeared completely from the landscape.

Some villages, such as Elton, just west of Stockton-on-Tees, have shrunk in size, with modern homes dotted along the roadside close to the parish church of St John. Largely rebuilt in 1841, the church retains a Norman doorway and Norman chancel arch with beak head decoration, and during the early medieval period it served a much larger community that spread into fields on the north and south sides of the roadway through the village.

A few miles further north, on the route from Stockton to Sedgefield, stood the prosperous township of Layton. It continued as a thriving market centre

An archaeological dig in progress at Layton during November 1978.

Above: Farm buildings at Swainston close to the site of the deserted medieval village.
Right: The site of the deserted medieval village of Swainston.

throughout the medieval period and into the late sixteenth century, when the site was referred to as Layton Graves. Traders passing along the route from Newcastle to Stockton via Sedgefield and Blakeston Lane stopped off at Layton, but its end was signalled when the area was purchased for sheep farming and people and properties were swept away. Today the outlines of buildings below the turf are all that remain of this once busy trading centre.

It was a similar story at nearby Embleton and Swainston, which virtually disappeared during the late sixteenth century. No record exists of them after about 1600 and evidence uncovered during excavations at Swainston in the late 1950s pointed to a period of prosperity covering the fourteenth and fifteenth centuries. Sheep farming, it seems, replaced long-standing agricultural communities, but at Embleton the last vestiges of the village survived until recent times. The Anglican church closed its doors in 1964, an inn formerly occupied two altered domestic properties and a pear tree marked the site of the schoolmaster's orchard with adjacent school buildings.

Inset above: Derelict farm buildings at Embleton.

Above: Embleton church, one of the few remaining buildings in the village.

Garmondsway covers a north-facing slope about a mile south-east of Coxhoe, with a series of well-preserved earthworks marking the outlines of this deserted medieval village site. According to tradition, King Canute and his retainers walked barefoot and bareheaded from here into Durham City, a distance of 7 miles, to do penance at the shrine of St Cuthbert.

Claxton, close to Hartlepool, is a medieval moated site, and items recovered during excavations in 1983 included two leather soles and a wooden and iron weeding hook.

Mystery surrounds the twelfth-century church of St Thomas Becket at Grindon near Thorpe Thewles, known as Grindon Priory. It is noted for its rare Gothic style and may have been the first church in the country to be dedicated to St Thomas after his canonisation in 1172. Local folklore suggests that an enterprising Bishop of Durham became so concerned about the number of people making pilgrimages to Canterbury Cathedral after the murder of Becket that he took items of stonework covered with the blood of the priest and had them incorporated into several churches.

Grindon Priory near Thorpe Thewles.

The porch and entrance to Grindon Priory.

The church fell into disuse after the locality's main benefactors, the Londonderry family, built a new church at Thorpe Thewles in 1848–9. So far there is no firm evidence of a village settlement at Grindon within the immediate area of the church, but survey work at two neighbouring sites close to the Tees has provided a fascinating insight into the fate of once-thriving medieval settlements. Newsham is located between Middleton One Row and Aislaby, overlooking the Tees, while West Hartburn lies between Darlington and Egglescliffe (some 2½ miles south-west of Long Newton).

Newsham was well established by the late eleventh century and comprised between eighteen and twenty-five homesteads. By 1390 one man owned the whole site and this indicates that depopulation had taken place during the fourteenth century. Aerial surveys have shown that the house sites would have had clay walls on stone foundations, with clay boundary walls in the gardens.

A sunken road runs the full length of the village and leads down a steep bank to the River Tees, where livestock would be watered. Again it seems that sheep farming replaced human occupation, with the only remaining buildings being Newsham Hall, with parts dating from the seventeenth century, and the former chapel, which was used in recent years by the local branch of the Women's Institute.

The village of West Hartburn was excavated during the summer months of 1962, 1965 and 1968, when three medieval homesteads were closely surveyed. Buildings ranged along a narrow village green and periods of occupation covered the thirteenth to sixteenth centuries. Items recovered included amounts of thirteenth-century pottery, and archaeologists also uncovered flagged causeways leading from the houses to a well. While East Hartburn prospered on Stockton's western perimeter, the village of West Hartburn disappeared almost into oblivion.

History repeated itself in a twentieth-century industrial setting with the development of Graythorp village on a 100-acre site during 1920–1. Housing was constructed by William Gray & Co. of West Hartlepool for the workforce, and their families, employed at the nearby shipyard on the north side of the Tees estuary. The yard concentrated mainly on shipbuilding, with repair work as

Housing at Graythorp village.

Industry surrounding Graythorp village, which resulted in demolition and clearance.

The site of Graythorp village after demolition of the whole township.

a secondary enterprise, while the new township with neat houses and gardens was surrounded by open fields. Former residents recall a church service in one home and outings by rowing boat from Graythorp into nearby Greatham Creek. However, by the 1970s industry had closed in around this homely setting, and completion of an adjacent industrial-tank farm signalled the end for Graythorp. In the late summer of 1979 an inquiry ruled in favour of demolition and clearance of the whole site and by 1983 the whole village had been removed. After little more than sixty years of existence, Graythorp village disappeared and the site has since been redeveloped as an industrial estate.

A similar sequence of events took place at Haverton Hill, where the Furness shipyard was opened in 1917 on 85 acres of reclaimed land. A model village of 564 houses was completed nearby to accommodate the workforce and in 1930 the offices of the Billingham Urban District Council were opened in the locality. Industrial development on this sector of the north bank of the Tees brought intolerable levels of pollution, resulting in demolition of the council offices in 1968 and clearance of housing during the 1970s.

Down the centuries Stockton-on-Tees has enjoyed varying fortunes, and one prosperous phase in the town's history brought the demise of a set of buildings that dominated the local townscape for some 500 years. At the end of the seventeenth century the Bishop of Durham's castle and adjacent parkland disappeared almost without trace.

A manor house owned by the Bishop of Durham is mentioned in the Boldon Book, a survey of land holdings in the county of Durham, in 1183, but the discovery of stonework dating from between 1150 and 1170 indicates an earlier building on the site. These early premises were obviously of some merit, as King John stayed here in 1246 when he granted a charter to the burgesses of Newcastle. Soon afterwards, in 1249, Bishop Farnham retired to Stockton and lived in these riverside quarters until his death in 1257.

The buildings were surrounded by a moat, which was probably completed in the early thirteenth century and in all likelihood served as an aid to drainage of the area or as fish ponds. First mention of the castle appears in 1376, when one of the bishop's wards was abducted. Account rolls for the late-fifteenth and early sixteenth centuries give details of spending on the various buildings, which included 'a great barn', a common furnace and a bakehouse. In addition, there were a riverside staithe (built in 1515 at a cost of £7 17s 11d) and a chapel, where ordination ceremonies for up to forty people took place each September between 1532 and 1535.

During 1543 King Henry VIII garrisoned troops at Stockton Castle, and, although the buildings seem to have been in a state of disrepair by the mid-1570s, they were sufficiently comfortable to allow the ordination of eight priests and eight deacons by Bishop Barnes in 1586 and to accommodate Bishop Matthew, who fled to Stockton in 1597 when the plague broke out in Durham.

THIS STONE COMMEMORATES
THE RE-OPENING OF THE OLDEST
SURVIVING GEORGIAN THEATRE,
ORIGINALLY OPENED IN 1766.
RE-OPENED BY COUNCILLOR
JIM COOKE, MAYOR 29 APRIL 1980

Stone from Stockton Castle was dispersed around the town and used in later
buildings including (in all probability) the Georgian theatre of 1766.

In 1640 Stockton Castle was again garrisoned by the king's forces and was considered significant enough to be excluded from areas handed over by the terms of the Treaty of Ripon. Following the victory of parliamentary forces at Marston Moor, Stockton was occupied by Scottish troops under the Earl of Callander in August 1644 and they stayed until 1647.

An Order of Parliament made during 1647 signalled the castle's demise, with instruction for its removal and, following the sale of the site to William Underwood and James Nelthorpe for £6,175 10s 2½d in 1648, Stockton Castle was totally demolished during 1652.

Remarkably, almost every trace of this impressive set of buildings soon disappeared with the erection of two ivy-clad cottages and then the Castle Buildings and adjacent brewery. Stonework from the old castle was dispersed throughout the district as the town entered a phase of redevelopment during the late seventeenth century. Buildings in Finkle Street, on the east side of Stockton High Street, and in Hartburn village may well have been constructed from stone from the castle site. One item of masonry, the Lion Stone, has been commonly known as the only identifiable remains of Stockton Castle and acquired a chequered history of its own.

It turned up in a farmyard at Hartburn, from where it was removed to Colonel Sleight's residence at nearby Elton. Here it was found in the early 1920s, in Crow Wood, marking the burial place of a famous racehorse named Othello. Subsequently this fine item of carved stonework was installed in the vestibule of old Borough Hall, but when this building was demolished to make way for the Odeon cinema and general post office in the early 1930s the Lion Stone disappeared among the debris. During 1952 it was rediscovered in a heap of rubble at the north end of the lake in Ropner Park and is now located in Stockton's Green Dragon Museum.

Other tangible reminders of Stockton's heyday under the influence of successive bishops of Durham are few and far between, but the town's insignia, a castle and anchor, provides an enduring reminder of earlier glories.

Further along the Tees Valley, west of Darlington, the glory days of Piercebridge were hidden for almost 2,000 years before excavations uncovered a dramatic insight into a much earlier period of occupation. During AD 70 Roman legions launched an attack on the Brigantian stronghold at Stanwick and opened up a supply route along Dere Street, with a settlement around the river crossing point at Piercebridge. An agricultural community developed, along with a copper-working industry and a *vicus* (civilian settlement) close to the permanent military presence, and, although an early bridge was washed away during a flood in the middle part of the second century, this was soon replaced.

A new fort was constructed in about AD 300 with strong outer defence walls enclosing about 10½ acres; the present village of Piercebridge was built within these perimeter walls. In 1933 a latrine building was discovered in the north-

A reminder of Stockton Castle appears on the castle-and-anchor insignia
(shown here on the town hall at the centre of the marketplace).

east corner of the fort, but the extent and importance of the Roman settlement
was not appreciated until excavations in the late 1970s uncovered a range
of buildings along the eastern side of the village. These remains have been
consolidated and are open to the public with access from a lane alongside St
Mary's Church.

On the opposite side of the river, close to the former site of the vicus, the piers
and abutments of the Roman bridge have also been exposed and consolidated
for public viewing. (An alternative theory has been put forward by Raymond
Selkirk, suggesting that the stonework was, in fact, part of a canal system linked
to the river.)

Associated buildings such as a water mill and temples were located around
the settlement's northern perimeter at a time when Piercebridge was one of the
Roman Empire's most impressive northern frontier bases, but there are few signs
in the early twenty-first century of these earlier imperial glories.

Index of Place Names